Leading in the
Digital Environment

Leading in the Digital Environment

Being a Change Agent

Edited by Lin Carver
and Holly S. Atkins

ROWMAN & LITTLEFIELD
Lanham • Boulder • New York • London

Published by Rowman & Littlefield
An imprint of The Rowman & Littlefield Publishing Group, Inc.
4501 Forbes Boulevard, Suite 200, Lanham, Maryland 20706
www.rowman.com

6 Tinworth Street, London SE11 5AL, United Kingdom

British Library Cataloguing in Publication Information Available

Library of Congress Cataloging-in-Publication Data
Names: Carver, Lin, 1955– editor. | Atkins, Holly S., 1958– editor.
Title: Leading in the digital environment : being a change agent / Edited by
   Lin Carver and Holly S. Atkins.
Description: Lanham : Rowman & Littlefield Publishing Group, [2021] |
   Includes bibliographical references. | Summary: "This book focuses on
   effective technology use and diffusion"— Provided by publisher.
Identifiers: LCCN 2020048586 (print) | LCCN 2020048587 (ebook) |
   ISBN 9781475859225 (cloth) | ISBN 9781475859232 (paperback) |
   ISBN 9781475859249 (epub)
Subjects: LCSH: Educational leadership—Data processing. | Education—
   Effect of technological innovations on. | Educational technology.
Classification: LCC LB2806.17 .L42 2021 (print) | LCC LB2806.17 (ebook) |
   DDC 371.33—dc23
LC record available at https://lccn.loc.gov/2020048586
LC ebook record available at https://lccn.loc.gov/2020048587

This book is dedicated to all the leaders who make a difference in the lives of students every day.

Contents

Preface   xiii

Acknowledgments   xvii

1 Creating a Culture of Investigation   1
       Holly S. Atkins, Nakita Gillespie, and Kimberly Higdon
       Foundational Elements—The 4 Ts 3
         Tools 3
         Training 4
         Time 4
         Teams 4
         Leadership 5
       Collaborative Community 5
       Building the Team 5
       Vision and Common Purpose 6
       Begin with the Willing 7
       Role of Trust in a Collaborative Culture 8
       Teacher Communities of Inquiry 9
       Inquiry Is What We're Doing Each Day 10
       Supporting Teachers in Asking the Right Questions 11
       Writing the Question 13
       Implementation Plan 14
       Plan for Data Collection and Reflection 14
       Flexibility in Response to Data Reflection 15

Building Capacity for Teacher Leadership 15
What Can This Look Like? 16
   Building on Existing Structures: Professional
     Learning Communities 16
   Again—It's about the Questions 17
   Rapid-Fire Inquiry: Tech Shoot-Outs 18
   Sustained Teacher Inquiry: The Teacher Technology
     Summer Institute 18
   Sample Inquiry Projects from the Teacher
     Technology Summer Institute 19
   Technology Innovations in Collaborative
     Communities 19
Conclusion 20
Reflect and Apply Activities 21
References 21

2   Digital Access and Ethics   25
Monica Iles

Theoretical Background 25
Ethical Standards and Implications 26
Student Privacy 27
Technology Safety 29
Equity and Access 31
Leadership Considerations with Technology 32
Reflect and Apply Activity 33
References 33

3   Using Technology to Enhance Profession Learning   35
Rachel Hernandez

Theories That Support Technology Use to Enhance
   Professional Learning 38
   Teacher Self-Efficacy 38
   Technological Pedagogical Content Knowledge 39
Administrative Support 40
Utilizing Technology for Professional Development 43
   Choice-Based Professional Development 43
   Online Courses 44
   Video Coaching 44
   Simulations 45
Professional Learning Networks 46

Reflect and Apply Activities 48
References 49

4 Writing in a Digital Environment   51
Elisabeth Denisar

Where to Begin 52
The Writing Process: The Foundation for Writing
    Instruction 52
Does Digital Writing Matter? 54
Capitalizing on "Old" Modes of Writing for Digital
    Writing 56
The Writing Process: Innovation Is Not the Enemy
    of Instruction 57
Prewriting/Inquiry 58
Drafting 58
Revising 59
Proofreading/Editing 59
Feedback/Conferencing 60
Publishing 60
Conclusion 62
Reflect and Apply Activities 62
References 63

5 Digital Wellness in Our Schools   65
Brandy Pollicita

Introduction 67
Youth Digital Landscape 68
Wellness as a Model for Digital Intervention 71
Tech Effects on Youth Wellness: "Expectation
    versus Reality" 72
    Physical Health 73
    Emotional Well-Being 74
    Productivity 76
    Relationships and Communication 77
    Character and Identity 78
    Personal Safety 79
Digital Wellness Roots and
    Recommendations 80
Reflect and Apply Activities 84
References 84

6   The Role of Coding   89
     Madison McClung

     What Is Coding? 90
     How to Get Started with Coding 91
     Teaching for the Twenty-First-Century Student 92
     Curriculum Integration 93
     Noncomputer Coding Alternatives and Coding
        Movements 95
     Conclusion 97
     Reflect and Apply Activities 98
     References 98

7   Breaking Down Barriers to Achievement through
     Universal Design for Learning and Assistive Technology   101
     Lori Goehrig, Maureen Kasa, and Jessie Brown

     Instructional Technology and Universal Design for
        Learning 102
     Assistive Technology for Students with Disabilities 103
     Instructional and Assistive Technology Solutions
        for Students with Learning Disabilities 105
     Assistive Technology Solutions for Students
        with Communication Disorders 106
     Assistive Technology Solutions for Students
        with Sensory Disorders 109
     Assistive Technology Solutions for Students
        with Significant Cognitive Disabilities 110
     Assistive Technology Solutions: Community
        Partners 112
     Conclusion 113
     Reflect and Apply Activities 114
     References 115

8   Visual and Auditory Production   117
     Lin Carver and Lauren Pantoja

     Multisensory Production 119
     Visual Production 120
     Auditory Production 123
     Question/Review Production 125
     Portfolios Production 126

Conclusion 127
Reflect and Apply Activities 128
References 128

9 Enhancing Social and Emotional Learning
   through Technology   133
   Lin Carver and Lauren Pantoja
   Social/Emotional Resources 134
   Social Emotional Concerns 135
   Culturally Responsive Teaching 136
   Benefits of Social-Emotional Learning 137
   Technology as a Bridge 139
   Technology for Young Children 140
   Technology for School-Age Students 141
   Technology for Teens 142
   Technology to Support Individual Learning 143
   Technology to Support Class Learning 144
   Conclusion 145
   Reflect and Apply Activities 146
   References 146

Index   151

About the Contributors   157

Preface

"I have a question for you," the principal casually asked one of her teachers as they walked away from bus duty. "There's teachers in the school using tech in great ways. How do you get *everybody* on board?" Perhaps that question resonates with you. Much has been written on the subject of technology diffusion, the process where the enthusiasm and practices of early adopters spread to others. While elements of diffusion are woven within this text, the central focus is on the educational leader as a change agent.

In *Preparing to Lead in a Digital Environment*, we presented foundational principles and practices to support educational leaders in establishing K–12 communities in which meaningful learning with technology happens. *Leading in a Digital Environment* builds upon that foundation to address the how and why of "getting everybody on board." The two books can certainly be read as companion texts, but this is not a requirement. Readers of both texts will see similarities in terms of theoretical perspective and structural layout. Themes are recursive. Scenarios are presented to invite the reader into the shoes of fellow educational leaders. Activities end each chapter.

THEMES WITHIN AND AMONG CHAPTERS

Your walk through this text does not need to follow a specific path. While the chapters are arranged in numerical order with a sense of how to unfold the topics to best benefit the reader, in reality the book chapters can be approached in whatever order suits the reader. Often, we gravitate to a chapter title that resonates with us and our current thinking or situation. We grow as technology leaders not through acquiring a discrete set of skills in a specific order of progression, and so the reader will find in these pages new insights from one chapter often picked up and connected to in another.

Here's what lies ahead. The book begins in chapters 1, 2, and 3 with invitations for teacher leaders to consider the foundational principles of school culture, digital access and ethics, and using technology to enhance professional learning. Chapters 4, 6, and 8 engage the reader in stepping into the K–12 classroom to imagine environments in which technology furthers student achievement through writing and coding, as well as visual and auditory production. Chapters 5 and 9 focus on the affective aspects of technology leadership in considering the topics of digital wellness and the role of technology in enhancing social and emotional learning.

CHAPTER COMPASS

To guide the reader in their journey of preparing to lead in a digital age, a chapter compass may prove helpful. This compass leads the reader on a patterned path, a repeated structure. Each chapter begins with a real-world scenario, presented as an opportunity for the reader to step into the shoes of a fellow educational-leader facing familiar challenges of teaching and leading in a digital age. The scenario is extended beyond a brief vignette, serving as a thread to connect foundational principles to real-world applications. The scenarios also offer the reader the opportunity to deeply engage in the type of decision-making all effective leaders employ. This intentionality as a digital leader is particularly emphasized in these scenarios.

Each chapter concludes with a series of "Reflect and Apply Activities" designed to support our goal of a text that promotes the growth of the digital leader. The reader is encouraged to engage in those activities to deepen their understanding of theory in application.

TO JOURNEY ALONE OR WITH TRUSTED COMPANIONS?

Is there a right or wrong way to read a text? Of course not. As coeditors of a text filled with chapters written by coauthors, our collaborative nature is clear. And so yes, we could see the text as part of a professional learning community. We hope the scenarios woven throughout the text provide leaders with an important lens to reflect on their current practices and set goals for future ones. And yes, the text may be part of a course syllabus so that the classroom community forms the collaborative structure. But perhaps you pick up this text and read it on your own. The leaders in each chapter become your trusted companions. Walk their walk as you reflect on your own.

WITH GRATITUDE

As coeditors of *Leading in a Digital Age*, we acknowledge that the text literally would not have been possible without our colleagues whose voices, expertise, and daily lived experiences as educational-leaders form the practitioner-based foundation of this book. We are grateful for their willingness to say "yes" to our gentle request to add one more item to their overflowing plates. Thank you, all.

Acknowledgments

Our most sincere thanks to Carlie Wall and the editorial staff for going above and beyond to make this book a success.

Chapter 1

Creating a Culture of Investigation

Holly S. Atkins, Nakita Gillespie, and Kimberly Higdon

Picture this: your distinct mandates a hot, new technical advancement meant to revolutionize education. They invest in equipment for all the classrooms and perhaps even a quick training session at the beginning of the school year. Teachers are not sold on the tool and are not willing or able to invest much time in investigating how to use it productively. By the end of the school year, perhaps a few teachers have embraced the technology, but for the most part, teachers have tried it once or twice and abandoned the new tool, or even worse, never opened the box of equipment, and the tools gather dust and take up space as they grow obsolete. Most likely, every experienced educator has witnessed this at least once.

Does it have to be this way? Consider an alternative scenario. Karen is a principal at N. O. Vate School, and like every other school leader and teacher, she wants to leverage technology to increase student achievement. Instead of starting with the magic tool (spoiler—there is no magic tool), she begins with talking to her teachers. She assembles a team of teachers who want to explore options for improving their practice. The teachers discuss their goals for students and describe what it looks like when students are meeting those goals. Karen questions and probes, and the teachers question and push each other to hone in on a specific goal—perhaps it is one goal, or perhaps the team splits into smaller teams to address a particular problem or challenge. The teachers then explore different tools. They may do some online research, talk to teachers in other schools, attend a workshop, or visit the exhibit hall of a professional conference. Karen facilitates this learning by coresearching with her teachers, organizing training with technology resource providers, creating the space for teachers to visit other classrooms, or finding funds for teachers to attend technology conferences. Once the teachers decide on a strategy or tool, they discuss how they will use the tool, and how they will measure success (or lack thereof) at different points over an agreed-upon time frame. Karen continues to question and probe to identify potential challenges or barriers and bring as much clarity to the process as possible. The teachers then apply their ideas while meeting periodically to discuss experiences, observations, and data collected. They share successes and challenges, and they problem-solve to get students on course to achieve their goals. Teachers might observe each other's classrooms, offering suggestions and gathering ideas for their practice. Karen is a part of this process as well, providing feedback, helping identify when teachers are getting offtrack from their goals, as well as problem-solving and facilitating practices that will help teachers and students hit their targets. As the year progresses, teachers are energized and feel empowered as they affect change and see the results. These teachers share their practices, both formally and informally, and generate excitement and enthusiasm among other teachers. The original teacher group continues this process, addressing more challenges, and helping facilitate this process with other teachers. Before long, Karen has garnered a critical mass of teachers who are actively examining their practice and using technology in ways that positively impact students' achievement and growth.

The following sections explore the process that Karen uses to cultivate the professional collection to effectively use technology to impact student achievement and to facilitate a faculty of empowered teachers who are actively involved in the development and growth of their teaching practices. The first sections address in a general sense how to build the professional community and the essential components needed for the innovative use of technology to support student growth. Following, the next section shares specific practices school leaders could adopt to facilitate the inquiry process among the faculty. Finally, the chapter concludes with a variety of models for how these practices can be applied in educational settings.

FOUNDATIONAL ELEMENTS—THE 4 TS

As an effective leader, Karen understands she needs to consider the foundational principles and elements that must be in place for her teachers to become genuine digital educators. Four critical, symbiotic components essential to the development of digital educators provide the foundation within which teachers can engage in inquiry that leads to effective technology use—the 4 Ts: tools, training, time, and teamwork (Roberts & Atkins, 2015) (see figure 1.1).

The Four T's of Technology Transformation

Figure 1.1 Four Ts

Each component is integrally connected and interdependent, leading to the technology transformation of teachers. Karen embraces her role as a school leader and understands the integration of these critical technology components within an environment of teacher-based inquiry and woven together by effective leadership will provide the foundation for formal and informal, short- and long-term structures for her teachers to integrate technology as a tool for inquiry and professional growth. Karen is aware that the omission of a component, prioritizing one element over the others, lack of leadership coordinating the parts, or a lack of a foundational environment of inquiry will result in ineffective technology integration.

Tools

Researchers have identified numerous barriers to effective technology integration (Francom, 2019; Heath, 2017). Access to technology tools, including equipment, Internet access, and network infrastructure, is paramount. When teachers have access to the technology tools, from hardware to software, they are more willing to experiment and investigate ways these tools can impact student learning. Karen knows, for example, if teachers are exploring an innovation requiring each student to have a tablet, only buying five tablets for the grade-level team and expecting teachers to adapt will likely not bear fruit. For technology innovation to occur, teachers (and students) need regular, sustained access to technology tools.

Training

Critical for Karen to bear in mind when considering her training offerings is that when the focus is on the tool and not on the pedagogical implications of using the device in instruction, teachers are less likely to use the tool for meaningful instructional purposes, if at all. Again, creating an environment of questions is critical. Effective support for the integration of technology is more professional development than simply providing training. Teachers need to be transformed, rather than merely informed (Darling-Hammond et al., 2017).

Time

A rare commodity in education is time. Without time to explore, create, and develop useful integration of technology tools, no real transformation can occur. As a component of professional development, providing time becomes a way to increase accountability. Professional learning communities (PLCs) should be structured to provide ongoing opportunities for inquiry, professional development, and progress check-ins to ensure that those best intentions for technology integration are put into practice (Yendol-Hoppey & Dana, 2010).

Teams

Collaborative communities of practice can support teacher development (Darling-Hammond et al., 2017) through technology integration and transformation (Anderson & Dexter, 2005). Karen has witnessed that teachers tend to attend training with others with whom they have established a collegial relationship. These relationships can provide the basis for intentional, collaborative communities of practice that are able to engage in systematic, meaningful inquiry to improve technology integration (Rogers, 2005; Kotter, 1996).

Leadership

Karen's training and experience as a school administrator has led her to understand the critical role leadership plays in her faculty's development. She understands, too, that the top-down approach is ineffective at best. And so it is with the meaningful use of technology as a tool to improve teaching and learning. The powerful, dynamic, and amplifying nature of the 4 Ts is dependent on committed, engaged, and intentional leadership (Anderson & Dexter, 2005).

COLLABORATIVE COMMUNITY

To maximize the impact of the 4 Ts, a leader like Karen needs to ensure that she has cultivated a culture of inquiry within the collaborative communities. In these environments, teachers feel free to identify concerns and problems they are facing, share them with their peers, question colleagues, clarify targeted areas for growth in their teaching practices, and share ideas and resources. These practices help teachers feel empowered to risk employing new ideas, strategies, and digital tools. Furthermore, the faculty needs to be comfortable sharing results, even when the integration of the technology did not go as hoped. To foster the practice of teacher inquiry in using technology, Karen is intentional in cultivating a collaborative community in her school. A straightforward definition of a collaborative community is a group of people working together toward a common goal. Like an orchestra, for a collaborative community to function at peak performance, a school leader acts as the conductor, intentionally building the culture while leading the members individually and collectively to bring out their best performance and meet the organization's goals.

BUILDING THE TEAM

Karen as a school leader needs to focus on who she is working with before she focuses on the actions of the group. In *Good to Great*, Jim Collins (2001) describes this as getting the right people on the bus before worrying about exactly where you will take the bus. The orchestra conductor assembles the players before deciding what songs to perform. The leader should assemble teams that are motivated by passion and purpose rather than compensation (Collins, 2001; Finkelstein, 2016). Most individuals would appreciate the value of intelligence when hiring teachers, but a principal needs to look for people who are creative and tackle problems in creative and unique ways and who demonstrate flexibility and the willingness to adjust plans if the situation warrants. To find the right people, leaders should be willing to take time in the interview process and perhaps see how a candidate reacts to an unexpected question in the interview process and tailor the process to the organization (Finkelstein, 2016). Karen seeks out these types of individuals when attempting to fill open positions.

In Karen's school, like most others, there are staff who were employed at the school before the new leader entered the scene. These teachers need to feel that they are valued and safe and that they are an essential part of the shared purpose of improving instruction through technology integration. Change can be daunting, and it is crucial to "build context and capacity within your community to take on ideas that don't feel threatening" (Finkelstein, 2016, p. 189). Developing technology goals with teachers is far superior to imposing goals and practices in a school community (Robinson, 2015). Robinson (2015) further suggests that starting with small, simple goals that can be achieved easily is an effective way to build collegiality among the teaching staff. The most important thing a new school leader can do is to build a relationship with existing staff that creates a sense of safety and respect. This is the foundation on which a collaborative culture can exist.

VISION AND COMMON PURPOSE

First and foremost, the leader needs to communicate a common purpose. Seemingly a simple concept, this vision is the glue that holds the community together and instills a sense of possibility, energy, excitement, and importance to a large number of people. This vision should be carefully crafted, by soliciting the opinions and building on the strengths of the group members. Using the orchestra analogy, the conductor builds on the strengths and talents of the musicians in the group to create a sound that is unique to the orchestra within the structure of the song being played. So while the vision of technology integration may be similar to that of other organizations, it is developed for the specific school, needs, resources, and buy-in from the community. Not only does the vision need to be well developed, but school leaders must consistently and clearly communicate the vision, for if the leader is not thinking about the vision or fundamental purpose, it is unlikely the team is either (Finkelstein, 2016). Any school or team within a school can get energized around a purpose. Furthermore, the common purpose can be the glue that binds team members when conflict arises. Even when team members disagree, do not like each other, or do not respect each other; typically, they can work together if all team members share and internalize a shared vision (Patterson et al., 2012). Creating and communicating the vision is at the core of leadership. Karen's vision does not include a picture of the exact tools her teachers will use to increase student achievement, but rather establishing an inquiring and critical community of teachers, pushing one another's use of technology in innovative and data-informed practices.

BEGIN WITH THE WILLING

One common mistake in technology integration is expecting every teacher to be on board with a new tool or teaching method and insisting on collaborative work before teachers feel safe enough to engage. This can create "killaboration," a state where conformity and low-risk taking occurs (Burgess, 2012). Instead, it may be better to start with a core group within the organization, those who see the possibilities in the vision and are willing to risk implementing something new and perhaps even carry a sense of playfulness or enthusiasm into their work (Robinson, 2015). To build this group, the leader needs to be intentionally inviting and ensuring that team members feel affirmed and a part of something bigger than themselves. Participants should be seen as capable, valued contributors, supported in their growth, and empowered to make choices about their actions with a voice in its direction (Finkelstein, 2016; Robinson, 2015; Schmidt, 2004).

Karen uses this approach. Instead of waiting for all her teachers to be on board with her vision (which was unlikely to happen), she started with the teachers who are excited about exploring technology with her. Once this group is assembled, she makes sure this group has the space, the resources, and the systems in place for the vision to be realized (Robinson, 2015). It is the energy and success of this initial group, the early adaptors, that can pique the curiosity of other teachers and motivate them to engage in their own practice of technology inquiry.

ROLE OF TRUST IN A COLLABORATIVE CULTURE

In the 1980s, Frank Smith (1988) claimed that one of the biggest inhibitors to learning innovations is that administrators not only do not trust teachers to teach but that systems actually circumvent the dedication and knowledge that teachers bring to the table. This is a concern. A longitudinal study of over 400 Chicago schools found that one of the key factors impacting student achievement was the level of trust between teachers and school leaders (Bryk & Schnieder, 2003). Studies continue to reaffirm the value of trust and collaboration in school effectiveness (Anrig, 2013; Kalenberg & Potter, 2014; Modoono, 2017). Not only does the trust need to be directed toward teachers, but it also needs to be reciprocated toward administration, and, ideally, between the school and the community (Bryk & Schnieder, 2004). To fully realize the benefits of collaborative inquiry, establishing a culture of trust is critical. Karen makes it clear to her teachers that she was open to them taking risks while using technology, understanding that as long as teachers were honest and open in using and responding to data along the way, they would be evaluated as successful teachers. When teachers experience challenges, Karen has to be open to their concerns and support them with a problem-solving approach.

So how does one build trust? It starts with the leader who makes the decision to trust then earns the trust of the faculty (Hurley, 2011). One way to start is to emphasize the alignment of goals and create a feeling of security and value. Factors such as integrity, honesty, authenticity, predictability, reliability, nonjudgmental respect, personal regard, and clear, regular communication enhance trust

(Brown, 2018; Bryk & Schneider, 2004; Finkelstein, 2016; Hurley, 2011).

Karen is intentional in establishing positive, fair, friendly, and possibly, most important, transparent relationships with her teachers while demonstrating integrity in all her interactions. It might be surprising to note that to stakeholders, integrity and honesty are quite often established when leaders are willing to engage in difficult conversations with people in an organization. For this to be a relationship builder, these difficult conversations must include a feeling of respect, optimism, and a common purpose (Modoono, 2017; Patterson et al., 2012). Using data checkpoints as the basis for critical conversations can keep these interactions nonthreatening and authentic. Karen is direct and upfront about her questions and concerns as teachers engage in their technology-based instructional practices, bringing the initial goals into the conversations and offering solutions and support in pushing teachers further toward progress in their goals.

Another effective way to build credibility with faculty is by being open to ideas they initiate. Even if there is some hesitation, voicing concerns but saying yes more than no can quickly earn the regard of faculty (Modonoo, 2017). Karen found that when she supported teachers' ideas she was unsure about, one of two things can happen: the technology innovations worked beyond her expectations, or she had an opportunity to direct teachers toward the impact on student achievement goals in an authentic and affirming manner. Either of these outcomes helped built trust between Karen and her teachers.

While building the professional teaching community may be the most critical job of the school leader, once that is established, the school leader needs to support, provide resources, and promote the development of skills to reach the school goals (Robinson, 2015). The next section describes leading teacher communities in the inquiry process that drives technology innovative practices that are effective in supporting student growth and school improvement.

TEACHER COMMUNITIES OF INQUIRY

Once a collaborative school culture is established, how can school-based leaders make the shift from ineffective technology training to helping teachers transform the learning experience through meaningful technology integration? First, a shift in thinking about technology must occur. Rather than beginning with a technology tool and providing technical training to teachers, Karen shifts this process and begins with teachers identifying their students' academic and behavioral needs. The group together selects possible technology tools to meet those needs and engages in focused inquiry to determine the effectiveness of the selected devices (McKnight et al., 2016).

The process begins with helping teachers recognize that they already routinely engage in an informal inquiry process, and helps them to explore their questions about their classroom practice. These questions become the starting points for technology integration. Meanwhile, school leaders build upon the existing concerns by encouraging the use of technology as a tool to help solve relevant challenges in the classroom. Effective school leaders support the development of an implementation plan and help identify ways to collect data and reflect on the effectiveness of the implementation.

INQUIRY IS WHAT WE'RE DOING EACH DAY

Teachers are no strangers to the cycle of inquiry. On the contrary, most teachers are engaging in inquiry daily. Teacher inquiry is the "intentional study by teachers of their own classroom practice" (Yendol-Hoppey & Dana, 2010, p. 98). Upon entering almost any classroom after dismissal, Karen is likely to hear informal conversation among teacher groups, reflecting on the events of the day. Teachers routinely engage in these organic conversations, discussing lessons that went well (or not so well), classroom management strategies that are proving effective for most students (but not meeting the needs of specific students), as well as general challenges they are facing in their classrooms. Yendol-Hoppey and Dana refer to this as a school's "back porch" (2010). Likely, colleagues are responding with strategies that have helped overcome such challenges. Moreover, teachers naturally abandon strategies that are proving ineffective, while reaching out to peers, blogs, or journals, for suggested strategies for addressing concerns. Throughout this implementation, teachers are continuously collecting informal data through student discussions, student interviews, and academic performance and reflecting on the effectiveness of the new strategy or implementation. The key is for Karen to value these conversations and utilize them as a launching point for authentic, collaborative inquiry. After acknowledging the teacher professionalism that is already present at N. O. Vate, Karen helps teachers identify examples of inquiry that teachers have informally engaged in previously. By doing this, she helps ensure teachers feel confident in their ability to engage in further technology inquiry. Her next step is to probe teachers to find the underlying issues causing the challenge and develop a plan for investigating it. During this process, she can encourage the use of technology tools and strategies to help solve the challenges teachers are identifying.

SUPPORTING TEACHERS IN ASKING THE RIGHT QUESTIONS

Most importantly, the inquiry process must begin with academic or behavioral challenges that are authentic to the teachers' own experiences rather than being based on an agenda from outside of the classroom. "It is important to inquire into an issue or study a phenomenon that is particularly relevant to your work . . . the personal relevance of the topic is an essential prerequisite when choosing an action research focus" (Sagor, 2000, p. 47). Once teachers identify a challenge, they should begin developing an inquiry question.

Before dedicating time to a particular technology challenge, Karen follows Sagor's (2000) recommendation of using the following questions as a sort of litmus test to ensure the question is worth exploring at length:

- Does it concern teaching or learning?
- Is it an issue of significant personal concern?
- Is improving this within your control?

Given the dynamic nature of the classroom experience, it can be difficult for teachers to pinpoint the actual root of a challenge they are experiencing. Teachers often need to talk through these challenges at length to find the specific problem they want to address first. While various strategies can be used to develop a focus for the inquiry question (Sagor, 2000), most important is for the teachers to be provided with the opportunity to talk through the question while a colleague actively listens and asks probing questions. This colleague should focus on helping to find the root of the problem to develop the inquiry question. Karen supports her teachers by asking probing questions to help them carefully examine their practice. Some questions that are particularly useful for initial inquiry investigation are the following:

• Is there something that keeps happening in your class that is particularly frustrating?
• Is there an area of content in which your students (or a small group of students) continuously struggle?
• What usually goes well in your classroom, but seems particularly difficult this year/at this time/with this group of students?
• Fill in the blank: "If only my students could/would _____ then _____."

Once teachers have identified the challenge, leaders like Karen can help them narrow the focus of their inquiry. By narrowing the focus, teachers can implement technology tools and strategies that are targeted directly at the challenge, and thus are more likely to have a positive outcome. Narrowing the focus is also supported through probing from colleagues. These questions can help pinpoint underlying issues:

• What seems to be the barrier to achieving the desired result? Or what do you suspect is causing the problem?
• What would you like to see changed/improved, specifically?
• What specific aspect of _____ are you interested in addressing?
• Is there a prerequisite skill that needs to be addressed to achieve the desired result?
• What tech tool could help overcome the challenge?
• Have you heard or read about tools other teachers have used to address this problem?

Once an inquiry focus is narrowed, and teachers have identified the specific change they are seeking, they will need to explore possible tech tools and strategies that can be implemented to effect change. At this point, collaboration and administrative support are more critical than ever. During this stage of the process, teachers draw from the collective experiences and expertise of their colleagues to explore tools and strategies for implementation. As teachers explore possible solutions, school leaders should encourage the use of appropriate technology tools to transform the learning experience. This will require some knowledge of the available tech tools. It does not, however, require the school leader or teacher to be an expert. Having a school or district resource map of available technology tools, subscriptions, programs, apps, and so on can be particularly helpful in matching classroom challenges with possible solutions.

School leaders can also support teachers by connecting them with others who can provide additional support with the selected tools. Karen decided to use an informal sharing process that encouraged authentic idea sharing among teachers at N. O. Vate School, called a pineapple chart (Gonzalez, 2016). As part of this process, teachers self-identify strategies and tools they wish to share and welcome colleagues into their classrooms for an informal visit. These self-initiated, informal visits enable teachers to see best practices and effective technology tools in action and to learn about the benefits firsthand. This allows them to determine if the tool or strategy will be a good fit for their situation.

WRITING THE QUESTION

After pinpointing the challenge and deciding on a strategy or tool to implement, the next step is to write the inquiry question that will guide the remainder of the process (Sagor, 2000). The question requires a level of specificity that focuses on the implementation and data collection to determine the effectiveness of the integration. In addition to considering the challenge and the intervention or tool, a teacher must identify the participant group. In some cases, a teacher may seek to inquire about an entire class group. However, at other times it may also be appropriate to work with a smaller group of students or even an individual student. Karen encourages a simple model to aid her teachers in formulating a question that will help focus their technology inquiry. In this model, teachers develop a question by thinking about their challenge + the selected intervention (with tech tool) + their participants (see figure 1.2).

Figure 1.2 Writing the Question

If a challenge has not been thoroughly explored, or a potential solution has not been thoroughly researched, it will become evident in this stage of the process. If a teacher has a great deal of difficulty at this point, it may be beneficial to return to the exploring stage for further probing and discussion.

IMPLEMENTATION PLAN

Once teachers create the question, they will need to develop an implementation plan. As part of this plan, teachers discuss how they will use the tool and how they will measure student success. Pragmatic considerations such as the timeline and frequency for data collection are also critical (Roberts & Atkins, 2015). Within collaborative communities of inquiry, intentional points of consideration provide safe environments for discussions about how the implementation is progressing, unforeseen challenges, possible solutions, in-process observations, and reflection on student progress (Zepeda, 2015).

PLAN FOR DATA COLLECTION AND REFLECTION

To determine the effectiveness of technology integration, teachers will need to develop a plan for data collection as part of their implementation plan. In many cases, teachers are able and should be encouraged to use existing data for this purpose (Sagor, 2000). Teachers often mistakenly assume that for "data" to be valuable, it must be formalized and quantitative. Knowing this, Karen reassures her teachers that there is a multitude of ways to check for understanding and that the data that are collected should be meaningful. She encourages her teachers to collect data utilizing formats such as student interviews, exit tickets, performance-based assessments, and observational data (Sagor, 2000).

Data collection is another ideal opportunity for the meaningful use of technology. Many technologies are available to collect, organize, sort, and analyze formal and informal data in more efficient ways than ever before. Karen recognizes that data collection and analysis can be a challenging aspect for her teachers. She supports staff at her school to help establish a plan for data collection that will be beneficial as well as manageable. Together, they explore apps that allow for surveys, video creation, journaling, digital portfolios, and more.

FLEXIBILITY IN RESPONSE TO DATA REFLECTION

Acknowledging and communicating to teachers the dynamic nature of the inquiry question, implementation plan, and data collection is a critical task for Karen. Frequently, the question evolves into something more specific, or after further exploration, a more appropriate technology tool is selected. Furthermore, initial data may not support the plan as originally implemented. Ensuring teachers that this is a natural part of the process will remove unnecessary pressure, allowing the inquiry to develop organically (Atkins et al., 2018). By continuing to collect data, and adjusting the plan as needed, the inquiry remains authentic for the teacher and the students.

Karen recognizes her teachers become apprehensive when the inquiry does not progress exactly as planned. To continue to build momentum, she decides to check in with her teachers, reassuring them that the process does not always go smoothly. She praises the teachers for their collaboration, reflectiveness, and commitment to student success. After all, the reason her teachers initially engaged in this inquiry with technology integration was to improve students' learning outcomes. She reminds her teachers of the trust she has in their professional abilities and encourages them to modify their plan as needed.

BUILDING CAPACITY FOR TEACHER LEADERSHIP

In addition to increased student achievement, using this process builds capacity for teacher empowerment and teacher leadership. With teacher attrition as one of the most devastating factors in a school, cultivating a community where teachers feel their voices matter, they see the results of their work, and their work is celebrated, teachers are much less likely to leave the profession (Grahn, 2018). Furthermore, teachers who want to grow often feel they must leave the classroom to advance professionally; however, teacher leadership experiences like these offer opportunities for professional growth without leaving the classroom, which can help teachers expand their professional skills and practice (Grahn, 2018). These teacher leaders can further enhance the school community by supporting and advocating for the vision they helped craft, facilitating buy-in from other teachers in the building, and guiding their colleagues in navigating change (Grahn, 2018). While the primary goal with this process is student achievement, leading this process for change can offer additional benefits. Karen, for example, has minimal turnover in her school, and when she does hire a new teacher, she has teacher leaders to help assimilate that teacher into the culture of inquiry.

WHAT CAN THIS LOOK LIKE?

Karen works with a sense of intentionality to create a culture and environment of questioning at N. O. Vate School. Building upon the collaborative nature of her teachers, Karen has established an environment of honesty and questioning as a process for growth. Now what? She wonders how she can continue to actively support her faculty in moving forward with using technology as a tool for professional inquiry into classroom practices. How can she offer her faculty opportunities to engage in meaningful professional development, rooted in inquiry, and resulting in using technology in pedagogically sound ways?

Building on Existing Structures: Professional Learning Communities

To help spread the culture of investigation beyond the initial group of willing teachers, the next step is to leverage existing PLCs in this same inquiry process, with a focus on meaningful technology integration. The membership and structure of PLCs may vary from school to school and from year to year. However, a PLC is defined by the *work*

rather than the *group*. The PLC is an "ongoing process in which educators work collaboratively in recurring cycles of collective inquiry
and action research to achieve better results for students they serve"
(About PLCs, n.d., para. 1). Since the goal of the PLC is ultimately to
improve student learning, this is the ideal scenario in which to infuse
authentic investigation that utilizes transformative technology.

Again—It's about the Questions

Effective PLCs are grounded in three essential questions: (1) What
do we want each student to learn? (2) How will we know when each
student has learned it? (3) How will we respond when a student
experiences difficulty in learning? (DuFour, 2004). School leaders
can infuse probing questions during each phase of the PLC cycle in
response to each of these questions to encourage investigation around
the use of technology. More importantly, the potential implementation
of the technology tool will be authentic and meaningful to each teacher
involved in the PLC. See table 1.1 for examples of sample questions.

Table 1.1   Guiding Questions for Inquiry

PLC Guiding Question	Sample Probing Questions to Support Inquiry with Technology
1. What do we want each student to learn?	• How can our team utilize collaborative technology to ensure shared clarity on the standards for learning? • What collaborative tools can we use to track our essential standards for learning? • How can we use available technology to become experts on the content we seek to teach?
2. How will we know when each student has learned it?	• What technology tools are available to help us assess our students more effectively/efficiently? • How can we use technology to help us implement alternatives to traditional assessment methods?
3. How will we respond when a student experiences difficulty in learning?	• How can we utilize adaptive technologies to help better meet our students' academic abilities? • What educational technology will support our intervention plan? • How can we use diagnostic technologies to get a clearer picture of a student's foundational knowledge?

Rapid-Fire Inquiry: Tech Shoot-Outs

Always looking to build upon and expand her teachers' professionalism as leaders, Karen brought in Tech Shoot-Outs as a part of faculty meetings. Based on the foundational principles of PechaKucha (Japanese for "chitchat") with 20 slides, 20 images, 20 seconds per slide (PechaKucha, 2020), Tech Shoot-Outs are a low-risk method for teacher-to-teacher inquiry-based technology professional development. Variations abound, but the basic premise is for presenters to select a technology tool they have used with success, create a slide with a visual and basic information about the tool, and then prepare to deliver 20 seconds of information about the tool. Slides are gathered together, with a timer set to change the slides after 20 seconds. Presenters gather at the front of the room, ready to present when their slide appears. One adaptation of the 20, 20, 20 "rule" is to gather teachers into teams. A slide appears with the team name, and team members step to the front of the room, ready to deliver their 20-second professional development. These rapid-fire, engaging, and energetic presentations are accessible to even the tech newbie. Bring on the tech tools for inquiry!

Sustained Teacher Inquiry: The Teacher Technology Summer Institute

Karen understands true professional development empowered teachers. Training provides information; while professional development is empowering. Based upon this critical distinction, Saint Leo University began offering the Teacher Technology Summer Institute (TTSI) to local teachers in neighboring school districts in 2014. Local K–12 teachers were accepted into this no-cost, invitational summer institute not based upon their tech-savviness, but upon their demonstration of an awareness of the importance of inquiry, of student-based use of technology, and of the cyclical nature of growth as a teacher-professional. Facilitators (one university faculty member and three K–12 classroom teachers) built the one-week summer institute upon the foundational principles of teacher inquiry: identifying students' academic or behavioral needs, selecting appropriate technology tools to meet those needs, and engaging in focused inquiry with data collection to determine whether indeed those needs had been met (McKnight et al., 2016).

The inquiry process began at a one-day pre-institute held the month before TTSI. Here, the inquiry foundation was introduced. Teachers were presented with an overview of action research, examples of previous teacher projects, and time to brainstorm individually and collaboratively to begin the critical task of developing robust, authentic questions. Many of the participants arrived on the first day of the institute with fully developed questions. For many others, the process was one of continuous development. Even those who ended the institute ready to begin their projects in the fall reported at the mid-year check-in that their questions had evolved and they requested help from fellow participants to further refine their questions and projects. This is the powerful, recursive nature of the inquiry cycle.

Sample Inquiry Projects from the Teacher Technology Summer Institute

Through the years, many questions have been investigated through the TTSI. Links to two of these are provided below.

• How Can Virtual Reality Be Used to Help Build Students' Content Knowledge Related to Science? http://bit.ly/2BO3PCU.
• How Can the Use of Yenawine's Visual Thinking Strategies Questions with Texts Affect Students' Abilities to Effectively Cite Textual Evidence through Collaborative Technologies? http://bit.ly/2ooFfB3.

Technology Innovations in Collaborative Communities

Various school districts have applied these principles effectively. When Dr. Aaron Spence became superintendent of Virginia Beach Schools, he began by speaking with groups of teachers all over the district. He noticed that their concerns did not align with the current district goals and so he built support for new goals by aligning with what teachers saw as challenges and with their suggestions for using technology to address student achievement. As the leader, Dr. Spence helped gather resources to ensure teachers had the tools they needed and gave them opportunities to participate in training to develop proficiency in using the tools. Once the goals were established, he started with anchor schools willing to engage in the work. Across the anchor schools, teachers participated in PLCs with groups of teachers from other anchor schools engaging in similar work. Teachers were provided with time to collaborate with their teams to explore ideas, share successes, and problem-solve their failures. Over time, the teachers in the anchor schools shared their work throughout the district, inviting teachers from the non-anchor schools to become involved with their PLCs and dispersed the knowledge and their effective practices throughout the district. The district's goal was that in five years, this would be the practice for all schools (Discovery Education, 2020a).

Fort Mills Schools in South Carolina began with a different approach. District leadership set the goal of increasing the engagement of their students and decided that using technology for STEM-related learning was the path to success. They garnered buy-in through district training and selected a pool of teacher leaders from applicants who wanted to participate. The district sent these teacher leader groups to visit schools in other districts to help the teachers decide how they would meet their district goals and provided equipment and training for them to do so. School leaders were trained to support these teacher leaders by encouraging experimentation, giving feedback, and facilitating goal-driven data-based decision-making. Teachers collaborated more informally through meetings and social media. As a result of this informal sharing of ideas as well as offering the opportunity to lead professional development through a variety of avenues, other teachers began to apply these practices in their teaching, and like Virginia Beach, using technology to increase student engagement and achievement dispersed to a broader group of teachers. Leadership at Fort Mills Schools hope these practices will eventually become the norm in their district (Discovery Education, 2020b).

CONCLUSION

The chapter began with scenarios presenting two experiences integrating technology in classroom instruction and continued by exploring how an effective leader can successfully lead her school through the process of inquiry in technology integration. School leaders need to understand the foundational principles that contribute to technology innovation: tools, training, time, teams, and effective leadership. Establishing the collaborative community requires the careful building of the teaching team, the ability to communicate, and the skill to garner buy-in on the vision and mission, starting with those willing to take risks and fully engage in the inquiry process by establishing a culture of trust within the school walls. Once this is established, leaders can facilitate the inquiry process by rigorously questioning the current conditions, beliefs about the reasons, solutions for the conditions, and steps needed to reach goals. Finding and providing resources is also a critical step in this process. As teachers take action, leaders continue to probe, problem-solve, and celebrate along the way providing opportunities for teachers to share the process. These practices can be applied in a variety of ways: formal and informal PLCs, summer programs, professional development, and district-wide initiatives. Leading teachers through the inquiry process in effectively integrating technology in instruction can have a powerful impact on schools through increased student achievement, enhanced teacher empowerment, and the development of a robust teaching force.

REFLECT AND APPLY ACTIVITIES

1.1. Incorporate the elements of the 4 Ts of technology integration and design an inquiry-based technology professional development opportunity for teachers at your school. Be sure to identify each of the 4 Ts and the leadership role you will play.

1.2. Create a brief needs assessment you would use to determine the strengths and weaknesses of the environment at your school setting in terms of a culture of inquiry into technology integration. Ask a school-based educator to complete the needs assessment survey. What are two recommendations you would make to support in developing an inquiry-based culture at the school?

REFERENCES

About PLCs. (n.d.). All things PLC. https://www.allthingsplc.info/about#:
~:text=Professional%20learning%20community%20(PLC),for%20the%20
students%20they%20serve.

Anderson, R. & Dexter, S. (February, 2005). School technology leadership: An empirical investigation of prevalence and effect. *Educational Administration Quarterly, 41*(1), 49–82.

Anrig, G. (2013). *Beyond the education wars: Evidence that collaboration builds effective schools.* Century Foundation Press.

Atkins, H., Gillespie, N., & Higdon, K. (2018, March 26–31). *It's about the questions, not the technology: A teacher-inquiry approach to technology transformation* [Conference presentation]. SITE 2018 Annual Conference, Washington, DC, United States.

Brown, B. (2018). *Dare to lead.* Random House.

Bryk, A.S. & schneider, B. (2003) Trust in schools A Core resources for school reform, educated leadership, 6016, 40–45. http://www.ascd.org/publications/educational-leadership/mar03/vol60/num06/Trust-in-Schools@-A-Core-Resource-for-School-Reform.aspx

Burgess, D. (2012). *Teach like a pirate: Increase student engagement, boost your creativity, and transform your life as an educator.* Dave Burgess Consulting.

Collins, J. C. (2001). *Good to great: Why some companies make the leap . . . and others don't.* HarperBusiness.

Darling-Hammond, L., Hyler, M. E., & Gardner, M. (2017). *Effective teacher professional development.* Learning Policy Institute.

Discovery Education. (2020a). *Case study: Behind the scenes of Virginia Beach Schools' 5-year tech plan.* https://www.discoveryeducation.com/details/case-study-behind-scenes-virginia-beach-schools-5-year-tech-plan/.

Discovery Education. (2020b). *Full steam ahead: How Fort Mills Schools instills engagement and passion.* https://www.discoveryeducation.com/details/full-steam-ahead-fort-mill-schools-instills-engagement-passion/.

DuFour, R. (2004). What is a professional learning community? *Educational Leadership, 61*(8), 6–11.

Finkelstein, S. (2016). *Superbosses: How exceptional leaders master the flow of talent.* Portfolio/Penguin Random House.

Francom, F.M (2019) Barriers to technology integration: a time-series survey study. *journal of research on technology in education, 52*(1), 146. http://doi.org/10.1080/15391523.

Gonzalez, J. (2016, September 25). *How pineapple charts revolutionize professional development.* Cult of Pedagogy. https://www.cultofpedagogy.com/pineapple-charts/.

Grahn, L. M. (2018). Teacher taking the lead: Increasing teacher retention through leadership opportunities. *The Language Educator*, Aug./Sept., 34–37.

Heath, M. K. (2017). Teacher-initiated one-to-one technology initiatives: How teacher self-efficacy and beliefs help overcome barrier thresholds to implementation, *Computers in the Schools. 34*(1–2), 88–106, doi: 10.1080/ 07380569.2017.1305879.

Hurley, R. F. (2011). *The decision to trust: How leaders create high-trust organizations.* Jossey-Bass.

Kahlenberg, R, D. Potter, H. (2014). A smarter charter: finding what works for charter schools and public education. Teacher collage press.

Kotter, J. P. (1996). *Leading change.* Harvard University Press.

McKnight, K., O'Malley, K., Ruzic, R., Franey, J., Kelly, M., & Basset, K. (2016). Teaching in a digital age: How educators use technology to improve student learning. *Educational Researcher, 48*(3), 194–211.

Modoono, J. (2017). The trust factor. *Educational Leadership, 74*(8). http:// www.ascd.org/publications/educational-leadership/may17/vol74/num08/ The-Trust-Factor.aspx.

Patterson, K., Granny, J., McMillan, R., & Switzler, A. (2012). *Crucial conversations: Tools for talking when the stakes are high* (2nd ed.). McGraw-Hill.

PechaKucha. (2020). *What is PechaKucha?* https://www.pechakucha.com/.

Roberts, C. & Atkins, H. (2015). Teacher transformation: The 4 T's of becoming a digital educator. In D. Rutledge & D. Slykhuis (eds.), *Proceedings of SITE 2015—Society for Information Technology & Teacher Education International Conference* (pp. 2554–58). Association for the Advancement of Computing in Education (AACE). https://www.learn techlib.org/primary/p/150351/.

Robinson, K. (2015). *Creative schools: The grassroots revolution that's transforming education.* Penguin Books.

Rogers, E. M. (2005). *Diffusion of innovations.* Free Press.

Sagor, R. (2000). *Guiding school improvement with action research.* Association for Supervision and Curriculum Development (ASCD).

Schmidt, J. J. (2004). Diversity and invitational theory and practice. *Journal of Invitational Theory and Practice, 10*, 27–46. https://files.eric.ed.gov/ fulltext/EJ728846.pdf.

Smith, F. (1988). *Insult to intelligence: The bureaucratic invasion of our classrooms.* Heinemann.

Yendol-Hoppey, D. & Dana, N. F. (2010). *Powerful professional development: Building expertise within the four walls of your school.* Corwin Press.

Zepeda, S. J. (2015). Authentic action research. In *Job-embedded professional development: Support, collaboration, and learning in schools* (pp. 99–123). Routledge.

Chapter 2

Digital Access and Ethics

Monica Iles

Ralph Sanchez finds an email in his inbox regarding a public record request. The former principal had submitted the paperwork. The district representative is sharing that the parent is indicating there is more communication between the parent and her son's past teacher through a digital app. Ralph is worried about whether the information is accurate. The teacher in question is innovative in his practice and often finds engaging technology to use in his classroom. He was one of the few teachers in the school who offered a digital environment to his students.

Ralph knows that all communication is covered by the Family Educational Rights and Privacy Act (FERPA) (1974) and that not all software is designed to protect students' information. He ponders how serious this situation could be and if there are any ethical considerations that have potentially been breached by the teacher.

THEORETICAL BACKGROUND

To help analyze the situation being presented, Ralph needs to assess several essential references to organizational ethics outlined for leaders and some federal laws protecting students. As a leader, he is familiar with AASA, the School Superintendents Association Code of Conduct, and the International Society for Technology Education standards. Additionally, he is also very aware of the FERPA

(1974) and Children's Online Privacy Protection Act (COPPA) requirements (Federal Trade Commission, 2020). While there are some references around technology with many of the national organizations, it is not always clear what rules organizations should follow with digital tools. In addition to these parameters, there may be specific district policies and procedures that he needs to consider.

ETHICAL STANDARDS AND IMPLICATIONS

To begin considering how different organizations support ethical decisions with technology, it is important to carefully review the leading organizations and their current verbiage within the context of technology. The following is a portion of the code of conduct taken from the AASA, the School Superintendents (2020) website, that could potentially apply to technology use:
The educational leader:

1. Makes the education and well-being of students the fundamental value of all decision making.
2. Fulfills all professional duties with honesty and integrity and always acts in a trustworthy and responsible manner.
3. Supports the principle of due process and protects the civil and human rights of all individuals.
4. Implements local, state, and national laws.
5. Advises the school board and implements the board's policies and administrative rules and regulations.
6. Pursues appropriate measures to correct those laws, policies, and regulations that are not consistent with sound educational goals or that are not in the best interest of children.

A review of these statements easily applies to any decisions or actions related to technology. It is essential for school leaders to carefully consider the implications of their decisions in regard to an individual student. Laws apply both in a classroom environment as well as in the digital environment. The best interest of children must be an underlying assumption in any policy, procedure, or practice.

Another nationally recognized source for digital learning is the International Society for Technology in Education (ISTE), which last updated its standards in 2016. Within its standard of Equity and Citizenship Advocate, it specifically states, "Education leaders cultivate responsible online behavior, including the safe, ethical, and legal use of technology" (ISTE, 2020b). This specifically references the requirement of educational leaders to be thoughtful on both how digital citizenship learning is provided to students and teachers and how technology access and use is safe, ethical, and legal in its implementation. Furthermore, each state has specific leadership standards at the state level. These standards typically address concerns for students, and many have some aspect of technology included in the language.

STUDENT PRIVACY

There are two federal legislative acts that apply to students' use and access of technology: the FERPA and the COPPA. These acts were designed and implemented to protect children's information and to provide a parental role in deciding how children's information is used and shared. It is important to consider the parent's rights when using student information and allowing students to access digital environments.

The FERPA provides parents and eligible students the right to access student records and seek amendment (U.S. Department of Education, 2020). It also requires educational institutions to obtain consent to disclose personally identifiable information (PII) except under certain circumstances such as when a school official has a legitimate educational interest, or at the request of a representative from an accrediting institution or an auditing organization. FERPA (1974) prohibits the dissemination of student information to third parties without written consent. An allowable third party is acceptable when the third party is part of the institutional system and abides by the requirements established within FERPA (1974). In Ralph's situation, the parent is indicating the teacher was using an independent app to communicate on student matters with the parent. This makes all of the correspondence within the app part of the student's record and, therefore, would need to be accessible in a public records request.

Additionally, the U.S. Department of Education (2015) created a Data Security Checklist for stakeholders to help with "data privacy, confidentiality, and security practices." The checklist refers to some essentials for organizations to consider. With today's digital environment, it is important to have policies in place and systems that specifically address student privacy concerns such as PII. Lack of secure practices allows for data breaches. Many businesses in recent years have been criticized for data breaches caused by poor security or hacking (Kiesnoski, 2019). There is an expectation that PII is protected by organizations that require this information. This same expectation exists for schools. Districts must maintain acceptable use policies and continual training around appropriate access with technology and essential information regarding the security of student data.

Districts should have established firewires and filters with all technology access. Security risks must be managed by the organization and steps taken to prevent and address potential hacking that could allow access to employee or student data. Log-in procedures must ensure adequate password use and authentication of the device user. Any student or employee identifier should be encrypted when electronically transferred. These systems are suggestions to encourage the safety of the data owned by school organizations. There is a responsibility of the organization to ensure protocols are in place to address the protection of data. As a school leader, Ralph must be aware of the rationale for procedures related to data and security, and he must ensure his school operates within these best practices to protect his students' information.

The COPPA was enacted by Congress in 1998 (Federal Trade Commission, 2020). It specifically was initiated to protect children under the age of thirteen and to provide parents with oversight of how personal information is used by a website or other technological entities. Schools should be notifying parents when a third-party organization is collecting or using student data. Third parties should not be using student data for commercial use without explicit approval from a guardian. Additionally, COPPA applies when a child attempts to post a video or photos online; parents should have the ability to allow or not allow the post. However, if the app allows a child to create a photo, and it is not transmitted, COPPA does not apply. Any website or app that targets children or teenagers should be aware of COPPA and its implications related to using or transmitting data. If an organization chooses to use an app or website for students, additional oversight of the design and use of data should be articulated in agreements to ensure compliance with COPPA. Ralph must ensure that any application or website used by his teachers does not collect or share students' PII. If consideration is being given to using a resource that would share PII, parents must be partners in this decision.

TECHNOLOGY SAFETY

Technology tools can engage students and offer a digital approach to learning (Singh et al., 2010). Presently, technology allows interactive communication through simulations and videoconferencing by both the student and teacher. Using these tools provides a strong base for engagement and learning. It also requires consideration of security, privacy, and ethical concerns. Technology safety becomes increasingly important both with the content provided through the tool and the ways in which the tool offers collaboration and interaction for students and the teachers. Additionally, monitoring of the tool is required to ensure safety within the digital environment. Another concern is that the online environment may place children at risk for cyberbullying, and in some cases, child trafficking (Seller & Narvarro, 2014). Ultimately, all tools need to be properly designed to ensure students' safety.

Collaboration is evidenced within classrooms through grouping students to work together on a project. Within the group an active role is assigned to each of the students. There are multiple benefits to collaboration identified within education; this includes both social connections and peer interactions that promote learning (Gilles, 2000). Another connection in collaborative learning revolves around content or problem-solving, which allows students to think through their thinking (metacognitive strategy) with their peers. Hattie (2009) identified multiple metacognition strategies as having a medium or larger effect size in connection to student achievement.

There are a multitude of technology tools available to allow for collaboration through a digital environment. When considering technology tools for collaboration, it is important to confirm that the technology company is able to address concerns related to both FERPA and COPPA. Often times, small organizations may have designed a useful app or website; however, the issue of protecting students was not considered in the design of the invention. A careful screening of tools and resources must be done by the school or district to ensure FERPA compliance. Avoiding collaboration tools is not advisable due to the learning benefits; organizations and users must take on the ownership of screening these tools and ensuring they are safe for students' use (Schrameyer et al., 2016).

Moreover, recently the challenges presented by the coronavirus pandemic and the conversion to nationwide online learning for education brought up issues related to safety and technology tools with parents. A particular tool, Zoom used for videoconferencing, had system issues related to hackers sharing pornographic, hate images, and inappropriate language during online meetings (Setera, 2020). Fortunately, features were added to an update from Zoom that allowed videoconferences to be protected through providing specific links, waiting rooms before admitting individuals to the online meeting, and password-protected meetings. Parents reacted with concern and questioned the use of the tool. Many districts eliminated the use of the Zoom app due to these concerns and the FBI acknowledgment of the problems. Districts maintaining the easy-to-use and reliable Zoom app provided guidance to parents on additional safety features within Zoom. Zoom also sent a patch to ensure all systems were set for the privacy features automatically based on the concern from parental stakeholders.

Another consideration of technology usage and safety is cyberbullying. Cyberbullying by definition includes any online "aggressive behavior that is intentionally and repeatedly directed at an individual who holds less power than the aggressor" (Vaillancourt et al., 2017, p. 368). Approximately 34 percent of students in the United States reported that they have experienced cyberbullying (Megan Meir Foundation, n.d.). This is a major concern because youth who are cyberbullied report higher levels of depression, anxiety, emotional distress, suicidal attempts, sleep problems, and health issues. Cyberbullying includes hurtful statements, videos, or images shared about another individual.

Seiler and Navarro (2014) conducted a study and found that cyberbullying has three unique components: (1) victims could not escape the aggressor, (2) there was an increasing number of bystanders, and (3) there was anonymity in online cyberbullying. With engagement in online learning, or the use of blogs or social media for students' interactions, a layer of monitoring and supervision for both the teacher and the parent becomes an expectation. Additionally, an identified intervention for cyberbullying is for parents to teach appropriate online behavior (Seiler & Navarro, 2014). This onus also applies to educators. Educators need to incorporate digital citizenship as part of the required curriculum. Providing instruction and expectations around technology tools and interactions becomes a part of the instructional process when technology is incorporated into the learning environment. Furthermore, websites or applications used for interaction should have some type of monitoring capability before posting, or minimally some way to capture the information that is being shared to ensure appropriate net-etiquette is being used.

Additionally, providing access to technology and the Internet to children exposes them to the potential dangers of the Internet. Approximately one in seven youths receives an unwanted sexual solicitation during online use (Mitchell, 2010). Litam and Bach (2017) identify trafficking in the United States as child soldiering, labor trafficking, organ trafficking, and sex trafficking. Human sex trafficking specifically focuses on sex acts through force, fraud, or coercion with a child under the age of eighteen. Social media accounts where children post personal information can allow for easy access for predators. It is important to recognize that dangers do exist and to talk to students about online predators. Counselors play a role in educating both parents and students about this concern. Furthermore, teachers need to know what to look for and when to report concerns.

In conclusion, the appropriateness of material and resources will always be an issue when working with students. This issue definitely applies to the online learning environments and technology tools. Teachers become owners of website and technology tool decisions when they incorporate them into their course content. The health, safety, and welfare of students must be considered with all curriculum content and engagement strategies.

EQUITY AND ACCESS

The ISTE standards for student encourage students' use of a variety of digital tools to design, create, and broaden their perspective, and to collaborate with others (ISTE, 2020a). It also states students should have an understanding of digital citizenship. To incorporate these standards, leaders must ensure students have access to the technology. Access includes having hardware, software, and Internet access. Additionally, it requires the leader to ensure students are proficient in how to access and use the tools. Leaders provide this support through designing a vision of instruction, which includes technology, advocates for resources, and provides the needed supports for technological access.

Schools must consider technology equity; this is often referenced as a "digital divide." In the United States, we see differences in access with technology based on geographic location, socioeconomic status, and race. Technology becomes a critical factor in career and life success, so integration in academics and access are essential for all students. The aspect of equity with access covers situations such as access to devices, access to Wi-Fi, low bandwidth, and technology proficiency. This also bridges over to parents' understanding of the technology use and how it impacts student engagement and prepares them for postsecondary or career success. Additionally, access may become an issue due to a student's disability. As a leader, any technology considered should provide accommodations for students with disabilities.

LEADERSHIP CONSIDERATIONS WITH TECHNOLOGY

Ultimately, in the situation with Ralph's teacher, it is unlikely that the application the teacher used was screened to determine the security of the student data. The use of the application in referencing students' progress or behavior makes the communication part of the student's public record. Additionally, any information placed in the application should be confidential and secure in complying with FERPA (1974). Procedures should be in place in any organization to ensure that technology usage is appropriate and used in the best interest of children, as well as complies with federal legislation when transmitting and using personally identifiable identification information. Leaders should have a plan to ensure access to devices and Wi-Fi, which allow students to engage at the needed level for later success. Technology should also be screened to ensure accessibility for students with disabilities.

REFLECT AND APPLY ACTIVITY

2.1. Review your school district's or setting's policies on technology and talk to the school administration or leadership about expectations regarding technology. Decide what areas need to be strengthened or developed around technology procedures based on the information presented in this chapter.

2.2. Consider the ethics and laws surrounding the safety and security of technology; what are the implications for leaders? How do leaders ensure staff are aware of the guidelines and provide technology access that complies with district and federal guidelines?

2.3. Consider the access to technology in your school, district, or setting. How successful is the technology integration? What types of access are a limitation for your learners? What strategies can be used by the district, administration, or leadership to ensure access is available?

REFERENCES

AASA, The School Superintendents (2020). Code of Ethics. https://aasa.org/content.aspx?id=1390.

Federal Trade Commission (2020). Complying with COPPA. https://www.ftc.gov/tips-advice/business-center/guidance/complying-coppa-frequently-asked-questions#General%20Questions.

Gilles, R. (2000). The maintenance of cooperative and helping behaviors in cooperative groups. *British Journal of Educational Psychology*, 70(1), 97–111.

Hattie, J. (2009). *Visible learning: A synthesis of over 800 meta-analyses relating to achievement*. Routledge.

International Society for Technology in Education (2020a). ISTE Standards for Students. https://www.iste.org/standards/for-students.

International Society for Technology in Education (2020b). ISTE Standards for Educational Leaders. https://www.iste.org/standards/for-education-leaders.

Kiesnoski, K. (2019). 5 of the biggest data breaches ever. Personal Finance. https://www.cnbc.com/2019/07/30/five-of-the-biggest-data-breaches-ever.html.

Litam, S. & Bach, J. (2017), "Otis": A case study of an online attempt to purchase children for sex. *Journal of Child Sexual Abuse*, 27(7), 806–17. https://doi.org/10.1080/10538712.2017.1360427.

Megan Meir Foundation. (n.d.). Bullying, cyberbullying, & suicide statistics. https://meganmeierfoundation.org/statistics.

Mitchell, K. (2010). Remaining safe and avoiding danger online: A social media Q and A with Kim Mitchell. *The Prevention Researcher*, *17*, 7–9.

Schrameyer, A., Graves, T., Hua, D., & Brandt, N. (2016). Online student collaboration and FERPA considerations. *Tech Trends*, *60*, 540–48. doi: 10.1007/s11528-016-0117.

Seiler, S. & Narvarro, J. (2014). Bullying on the pixel playground: Investigating risk factors of cyberbullying at the intersection of children's online-offline social lives. *Cyberpsychology: Journal of Psychosocial Research on Cyberspace*, *8*(4). Article 6. doi: 10.5817/CP2014-4-6.

Setera, K. (2020, March). FBI warns of teleconferencing and online hijacking during COVID-19 pandemic. https://www.fbi.gov/contact-us/field-offices/boston/news/press-releases/fbi-warns-of-teleconferencing-and-online-classroom-hijacking-during-covid-19-pandemic.

Singh, A., Mangalaraj, G., & Taneja, A. (2010). Bolstering teaching through online tools. *Journal of Informational Systems Education*, *21*(3), 299–311.

U.S. Department of Education. (1974). Family Educational Rights and Privacy Act (FERPA). https://www2.ed.gov/policy/gen/guid/fpco/ferpa/index.html?src=rn.

U.S. Department of Education. (2015). Data security checklist. https://studentprivacy.ed.gov/sites/default/files/resource_document/file/Data%20Security%20Checklist_0.pdf.

U.S. Department of Education. (2020). Protecting student privacy. https://studentprivacy.ed.gov/.

Vaillancourt, T., Farris, R., & Mishna, F. (2017). Cyberbully in children and youth: Implications for health and clinical practice. *Canadian Journal of Psychiatry*, *62*(6), 368–73.

Chapter 3

Using Technology to Enhance Profession Learning

Rachel Hernandez

Heart pounding, Katlyn Gomez arrived two hours early to Crestwood Pines Elementary School. Her enthusiasm for her new position as a third-grade teacher was in fierce competition with the nerves that caused her palms to break out in a torrential sweat and stomach to erupt in butterflies. Gathering her carefully crafted classroom decorations and recently purchased supplies for her new desk, she quickly made her way from the empty parking lot into the darkened halls of the school. An hour later, Katlyn heard a quiet knock on the classroom door. She carefully climbed down from her step ladder and away from her semi-decorated bulletin board. After opening the door with a welcoming smile, she was warmly greeted by Barbara Martin, the third-grade department chairperson. Barbara, a thirty-year teaching veteran, had experienced a great deal of changes over the years when it came to education. From the pendulum swing of educational policies to technology integration, Barbara was afraid for the future of her career. However, she was always eager to meet the first-year teachers that came to Crestwood Pines and enjoyed their newfound passion for the profession, as it seemed to rejuvenate her own fervor for teaching. For this reason, each year Barbara volunteered to mentor first-year teachers. She appreciated their quest to "save the world" one student at a time, while not yet being tempered down or jaded by the burdens of standardized testing and educational politics.

Over the next week of preplanning, Barbara worked with Katlyn on identifying and acclimating to the school practices of curriculum planning, state and district assessment preparation, data collection and analysis, and record-keeping protocol. Barbara explained that the testing and data could be a bit overwhelming since benchmarks are collected through computer-based testing, and most record-keepings, like student attendance and grading, are also kept through technology-assisted programs. The new principal of Crestwood Pines, Mr. Wayne, has been increasingly tasking the teachers to utilize the technology tools available to the school. Barbara was not fond of the excessive amount of technology trying to impede the classroom and felt fearful that one day it would take over the role of the teacher. The veteran teacher rarely utilized technology in her lessons as she found that it hindered the learning process. Not only was it a distraction, but it also required additional time and training for teachers to learn to successfully implement it into the teaching and learning process. Barbara quantified, "Teachers have enough on their plate already! The additional burden of learning to use new technology and then teaching the students to use and care for the devices is simply too much when we have the important task of preparing the students for state assessments."

This was on the opposite end of the pedagogical spectrum from Katlyn. As a Generation Z student who had just graduated from college, she reflected on the educational technology classes that she had attended while working toward earning her degree. Not only had she been taught the importance of technology integration for this generation of students, but she was also trained on how to effectively utilize this technology to enhance the teaching and learning process. Katlyn had a great zeal for technology and was eager to begin to utilize it in her classroom. She started to consider the contrast in her excitement and enthusiasm for technology integration with Barbara's hesitation and skepticism of technology use in the classroom. What factors contributed to this disparity? It was certainly not the generational differences or age gap; of this, Katlyn was certain. Katlyn's fifty-two-year-old father boasted of a "smart house," with every technological gadget known to the modern world. Not only were there cameras and communication devices inside and out but also the ability to control almost everything within the house with the touch of a button on his smartphone app. Furthermore, Katlyn's mother, also a veteran teacher with nearly thirty-six years of experience, utilized technology in numerous ways within her own high school classroom each day.

On the last day of preplanning, Mr. Wayne held a faculty meeting to address the state of the school before students eagerly began to fill the empty halls. After discussing the goals for the upcoming school year and any new programs that were going to be implemented, Mr. Wayne asked the faculty for their input as he wanted to address any questions or concerns. Barbara quickly raised her hand and began to question how and when teachers were supposed to begin using any new technology when they barely had enough time in the day to instruct students on the mandated curriculum. Mr. Wayne had tasked the teachers to not only utilize the computer-adaptive intervention programs during both math and reading blocks, but he is now also asking his instructors to use social media platforms for learning and communication. Mr. Wayne noted that several teachers shared Barbara's apprehensions. At this point, Katlyn raised her hand and nervously offered to help any teacher gain a better understanding of these programs. She stated that she was relatively familiar with these platforms due to her experiences in educational technology classes and interactions within her practicum and internships. She also went on to explain that her mother, a veteran teacher, uses them frequently in her own classroom.

After the faculty meeting, Mr. Wayne called Katlyn and Barbara to his office. He wanted to find out more about his teachers' perspectives and gather assistance from Katlyn by brainstorming the newest technology tools that would benefit the faculty and students at Crestwood Pines. He wanted Barbara's input on the overall perspectives of the other faculty when it came to the integration of educational technology. This discussion also offered ways to garner possible professional development training, since Katlyn and Barbara had offered their take on what they observed and witnessed as both a new teacher in the school and a veteran teacher leader who was trusted greatly by her peers. Together, they created a survey to identify the faculty's perspectives on technology integration. Some of the responses from this survey included the general feeling of being overwhelmed with the numerous tasks that the teachers needed to complete daily to ensure that their students were making annual yearly progress and preparing for the state assessment or the progression to the next grade level. Many of their peers felt as though they were not familiar with the new technology nor had the training to successfully implement these tools into the learning process. Others worried about the students misusing the technology or equipment not working or getting broken. There was a lack of consistency throughout the school. Some teachers used technology for numerous tasks during the day, while others still utilized a physical grade book and lesson planner. In the end, with the help of the survey created by Katlyn and Barbara, Mr. Wayne identified four emerging themes:

1. Teachers must believe in their own ability to guide their students' success.
2. Teachers must be familiar with and adequately trained in technology in order to utilize it successfully.
3. There must be consistency throughout the school when it comes to technology integration and training incentives.
4. Teachers do not feel as though there is enough time to be trained to integrate technology into their teaching.

THEORIES THAT SUPPORT TECHNOLOGY USE TO ENHANCE PROFESSIONAL LEARNING

Mr. Wayne was able to identify and understand the need for his teachers to be effectively trained in the technology that he wanted them to implement into the classroom. As an administrator, it is his job to ask his faculty to do what is necessary for the students of Crestwood Pines to not only be successful but also to help them to be college and career ready. However, simply giving teachers technology tools and computer-assisted programs to implement without first providing adequate training will not only cause frustration in his faculty, but it will also have a significant effect on *teacher self-efficacy*, or a teacher's belief in their own ability to guide a student to success.

Teacher Self-Efficacy

Teacher self-efficacy is a significant component of Bandura's social cognitive theory. This theory emphasizes human agency, or the awareness that people can exercise control over the actions that may affect their lives (Zee & Koomen, 2016). Within the social cognitive theory framework, feedback and positive reinforcement are important factors in the development of teacher self-efficacy. Therefore, it is crucial for Mr. Wayne to understand the importance of administrative support and teacher training when it comes to teacher self-efficacy and successful technology integration. Bandura (1977) explained that efficacy refers to an individual's perceived ability, which the teacher determines and is related to a specific task. Self-efficacy beliefs can affect a teacher's professional practices (Boulton, 2014). These self-efficacy beliefs will govern the way in which individuals feel, think, and motivate themselves to behave (Bandura, 2001). A person's perceptions or thinking about their ability is greatly connected to their motivation. This may be one cause for the reluctance in technology use in the classroom from many of the teachers at Crestwood Pines. What is more, teachers' self-efficacy is associated with students' academic growth and achievement (Brown et al., 2015). An educator's efficacy has been associated with their disposition and teaching practice and can also influence students' motivation, classroom management strategies, and increase academic instruction time (Woolfolk & Hoy, 1990). Factors that may influence teachers' self-efficacy when it comes to integrating technology into the classroom include the support of the administration and adequate training. The self-efficacy of teachers may determine their success, or lack thereof, in the effective integration of technology into the classroom curriculum.

Technological Pedagogical Content Knowledge

The next theory that Mr. Wayne identified as necessary to consider when training his faculty is the *Technological Pedagogical Content Knowledge (TPACK) Model*. This framework, designed by Mishra and Koehler (2006), helps teachers to understand the types of knowledge essential to effective teaching with technology (Chai et al., 2013).

Teachers understand each component in the TPACK individually. For example, *technological knowledge* is an understanding of the tools and materials, as well as the technical skills that one must utilize within the teaching and learning process. Emerging technology (software and hardware) as well as traditional technologies (books and blackboards) are included in this component. Teachers are expected to be knowledgeable about these technologies and should be able to effectively utilize them within their teaching and in all content areas (Mishra & Koehler, 2006; Pamuk et al., 2015).

Pedagogical knowledge is the art and practice of teaching or transmitting knowledge in a stimulating and motivating manner. Pedagogy refers to the effectiveness of teaching on students' learning. Shulman (1986) asserted that the principles and strategies of teaching, classroom management, learning, and motivation are components of pedagogical knowledge. Teachers must have effective classroom management skills, knowledge of teaching methods, understanding of assessments, implementation of appropriate structures, and the ability to adapt quickly (Mishra & Koehler, 2006).

Finally, *content knowledge* refers to the subject matter that the teacher wishes for students to learn. Within this component, the instructor must have an extensive understanding of the concepts, content, theories, and procedures to be effective (Mishra & Koehler, 2006; Pamuk et al., 2015).

The goal of the TPACK framework is the marriage of these three components. Some teachers may have a significant grasp on pedagogical knowledge and content knowledge, thus being proficient in pedagogical content knowledge. Other teachers who may be skillful in technology knowledge and content knowledge are considered capable of technological content knowledge. However, with adequate training, teachers could become proficient in all three concurrently.

Teachers can now create more TPACK as this framework gives educators specifications for the types of teacher knowledge necessary for effective technology integration (Koh et al., 2015). Teachers need each component of the TPACK framework to integrate technology into the classroom curriculum effectively (Cox & Graham, 2009). This knowledge is critical due to the emphasis on utilizing technology to foster pedagogical improvements that address the needs of students in a twenty-first-century world (see figure 3.1).

ADMINISTRATIVE SUPPORT

Based on the emerging themes from the survey responses from his faculty, Mr. Wayne was acutely aware of the need to address each

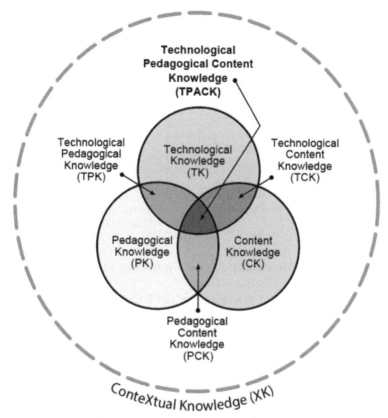

Figure 3.1 **Revised version of the TPACK image.** © Punya Mishra, 2018. Reproduced with permission.

issue individually. He knew that training his teachers was critical. He understood that the teachers of Crestwood Pines needed to feel supported and have a voice. Upon reflecting on the theoretical frameworks that support technology use to enhance professional learning, he created table 3.1 to map out his goals.

Upon outlining the issues or themes that needed to be addressed, Mr. Wayne found that teacher self-efficacy was a significant factor in the teachers' hesitation to utilize technology in the classroom. One substantial way to support teachers' self-efficacy is for administrators to assist teachers in feeling valued, confident, and successful. Through training and collaboration, the goal of *collective* efficacy, or when teachers believe that together they can grow and inspire change in their students, can be achieved (Boulton, 2014). Empowering

Table 3.1   Mr. Wayne's Map of Technology Goals

Emerging Theme from Survey	Contributing Factors
Teachers must believe in their own ability to guide their students' success.	• Teacher self-efficacy
Teachers must be familiar with and adequately trained in the technology in order to utilize it successfully.	• Professional development • TPACK knowledge
There must be consistency throughout the school when it comes to technology integrating and training incentives.	• Administrative support
Teachers do not feel as though there is enough time to be trained to integrate technology into their teaching.	• Professional learning networks • Self-directed training • Video coaching • Simulations

teachers to take leadership roles in the training process can assist in developing this collective efficacy.

Mr. Wayne could not deny the need for technological professional development for the faculty at Crestwood Pines. Since teachers' beliefs in their own abilities can impact their self-efficacy, it is imperative that teachers are effectively trained to increase confidence in their technological knowledge. With professional development initiatives, teachers can learn new ways to utilize technology to augment their classroom and enhance the learning experience for their students. Understanding that their pedagogical knowledge and content knowledge can be heightened through technological knowledge is critical.

Mr. Wayne realized that there was a lack of consistency and a "do what works for you" attitude with previous administration at Crestwood Pines Elementary. While some students enjoyed a technology-rich classroom experience, others were only offered an occasional PowerPoint that went along with the 300-page textbook. All students at Crestwood Pines deserved the best education possible. These students are Generation Z students. They do not learn in the same manner in which most of their instructors did. Generation Z students have unique learning preferences. They thrive on technology and tend to be more self-directed. This cohort of students' attention spans is an average of eight seconds, four seconds less than millennials, and they learn by observation and practice (Seemiller & Grace, 2017). These students do not prefer lectures but learn best by solving real-world problems (Shatto & Erwin, 2016). Since technology is a significant part of everyday life for this generation, teachers must provide a variety of innovative teaching methods across various platforms to keep them engaged (Williams, 2019). These multiple platforms include a variety of technology tools and programs. In order for Mr. Wayne to assist in addressing these unique needs of his Generation Z students, he must support his faculty by providing training on the technology needed to enhance classroom learning and engagement.

UTILIZING TECHNOLOGY FOR PROFESSIONAL DEVELOPMENT

With the overarching theme for improving integration into the classroom at Crestwood Pines being the need for training, Mr. Wayne considered the greatest factor for the reluctance to this technology integration. Most of the teachers felt as though there was little to no time for training. This would be the greatest hurdle for Mr. Wayne to overcome. How could he effectively train his faculty without cutting into the precious time they needed for planning and teaching?

Choice-Based Professional Development

Teachers need professional development to thrive. Mr. Wayne understands that each teacher has different needs, backgrounds, and strengths. Just as teachers are tasked with differentiating instruction, administrators must differentiate professional development. Differing needs require different forms and content in professional development (Wolpert-Gawron, 2018). Most teachers do not look forward to mandated professional development when it is less than high quality and takes away from the valuable time needed in the classroom. Technology plays an incredible role in offering teachers' choice-based professional development. The "one-size-fits-all" type of professional training is not a satisfying mode for teacher learning. Allowing faculty to have a voice in their professional development and offering a choice in the content and delivery will increase teachers' engagement and enthusiasm. Technology allows the focus to move to more active learning and away from the passive "sit and get" learning environment of the past. Consequently, Mr. Wayne began to research and identify ways in which his faculty could participate in meaningful training without having to sacrifice valuable class time.

Online Courses

The principal of Crestwood Pines identified online course offerings that teachers could take advantage of in the evenings, weekends, during the summer, or during the time that works best for them. Some topics of interest he identified included getting the most out of tablets, utilizing social media platforms for communication and engagement, and technology-assisted project-based assessments. When teachers have access to a comprehensive suite of webinars, they have the opportunity to pursue their own professional development at their convenience. As an added incentive, Mr. Wayne gave teachers "technology points" as well as professional development hours as an incentive to increase their knowledge about technology. These points could be accumulated and later used to redeem extra classroom technology tools (Peterson, 2019).

Video Coaching

Teachers need around fifty hours of training in any given area in order to improve their skills (Darling-Hammond, 2009). "One shot" professional development has been found to be ineffective, whereas continuous coaching can create a relationship between both coach and teacher. Technology allows for this to occur easily in that through video coaching, teachers can learn from one another. Not only do administrators seek to maximize the learning process for teachers, but they also want to make professional development a personalized experience (Huza, 2017). Peer-to-peer observations can assist in collaboration in classroom best practices. In the traditional classroom setting, finding the time to observe in another classroom can be a challenge. However, the use of video coaching allows for these observations without losing classroom time or distracting peers.

In order to allow teachers to have more time for planning and instruction, Mr. Wayne is looking to move to video coaching to not only assist new teachers in acclimating to the classroom but also to provide opportunities for teacher collaboration. New teachers can receive valuable feedback from mentors through the use of video. Administrators can also monitor instruction in the classroom with these recordings, which will allow them to pinpoint specific areas of strength and areas needed to have improvement. Teachers undergoing professional development training through professional learning communities (PLCs) can collaborate with their peers (Huza, 2017). They may share ideas through video recordings or asynchronous participation. Participants can even utilize video synchronously to collaborate live through videoconferencing tools. Many of these live tools can now share a given participant's computer screen, video or audio recordings, and other important documents.

When teachers are working with video coaches or participating in technology training through video, they have the opportunity to make connections to their peers and trainers. Instead of reading an email and responding via text, teachers can communicate in real time through synchronous video use or respond to questions by giving examples through classroom recordings.

Simulations

Simulations assist teachers and schools by cultivating the instructor's ability to improve the academic performance of students and advance the classroom management of teachers while also giving instructors the flexibility to complete their professional development at their own pace. Especially when it comes to first-year teachers, simulation programs can be ideal in providing the bridge between theoretical learning and practical classroom application. Simulations allow demonstrations of abstract concepts while the interactions within the simulations give feedback to teachers that will assist in improving their practices in a safe and effective manner (Lateef, 2010).

One such simulation program that Mr. Wayne is considering for his faculty training is Mursion. The Mursion program assists in building teacher confidence while also increasing competence and classroom skills (Virtual Reality Training Simulation Software by Mursion, n.d.). The Mursion simulation program offers learning opportunities for teachers by putting them into an immersive reality that allows teachers to interact in real time with a simulated group of students. This training simulation can be utilized to prepare teachers at every grade level for the challenges of teaching in the classrooms of today. The Mursion program was funded by the Gates Foundation and has designed new avatars that feature classroom interactions with general education students as well as with students with autism disorders, learning disabilities, and English language learners. They have also developed adult simulations where learners can practice parent interactions or coaching of other professionals (Virtual Reality Training Simulation Software by Mursion, n.d.).

PROFESSIONAL LEARNING NETWORKS

When individuals think of social media, they often reflect on vacation photos, selfies, deliciously appealing photos of food, or makeup tutorials. They do not often think about education, but teachers have an incredible opportunity to utilize social media to build professional skills. Social media platforms may be used to not only build those professional skills but also increase professional knowledge and build their network. When considering to utilize social media platforms for learning, Mr. Wayne will ask his teachers to consider three things:

1. What do they want to learn?
2. What do they have time to learn?
3. Who do they want to learn from?

Educators typically want to learn more about their profession. Thus, they must begin following leaders in the education industry on platforms such as Twitter or LinkedIn. Twitter offers a way for teachers to share ideas, network, brainstorm with peers, and build professional learning communities. Twitter also offers a way to connect teachers to one another and offers emotional support. Many teachers report needing ways to boost emotional support, identify needed resources, and foster professional relationships, all of which lead to increased resilience, a greater sense of identity, and fewer feelings of isolation (Carpenter & Krutka, 2014). Twitter also offers a way to connect to a global network of educators in order to solve a wide variety of educational problems. Research tells us that teachers value Twitter's personalized and immediate nature and the numerous ways in which it fosters positive collaboration among educators from all backgrounds and locations. This collaboration and emotional support may offset some of the problems of teacher burnout or educators leaving the profession way too early (Carpenter & Krutka, 2014). When exploring social media, it is important to begin by identifying what fellow educators are interested in. What do these educational leaders read and write about? What hashtags are they utilizing, and why? These hashtags will lead to resources that will be more like a road map helping teachers navigate their way to building their professional skills. These hashtags offer great resources for individuals looking for information related to specific concepts.

Blogs and podcasts are another effective way for instructors to increase their professional knowledge and skills. Educators should look to colleagues, identify what they are reading and sharing, and then seek out the best blogs and podcasts in the educational field (Ping et al., 2018). Many teachers at Crestwood Pines were concerned about how they would find the time to complete their professional development.

Podcasts are an easy and convenient way for teachers to quickly develop skills at any given moment. Listening to a podcast on a weekend walk, bike ride, lunch break, and even in the car on the way to and from work is a great way to utilize valuable time to bridge any professional gaps in skills. There is no need to plan additional travel time, spend time sitting in on lectures, or read lengthy books when podcasts are readily available for skill development (Felix, 2007). Not everything can be learned through a podcast, but Mr. Wayne was able to identify some examples of current podcasts, which included ELA podcasts where fellow educators described their thirty-minute process for planning reading units, shared practical tips for the classroom organization, presented ideas for increasing classroom instruction time, offered information on how to utilize Google apps, and proposed tips for increasing effective of transitions.

Mr. Wayne understands that self-directed professional development utilizing technology can assist in solving the issue of time constraints for building professional skills. The enhancement of these professional skills will increase teachers' self-efficacy and amplify the integration of technology at Crestwood Pines.

At the next faculty meeting, Mr. Wayne shared his new goals for the following semester. He placed Barbara and Katelyn in charge of forming a Technology Support Committee to work with teachers in creating plans for each teacher to identifying ways to use technology for professional development in their own time, understanding the importance of focusing on an area of needed improvement, one concept at a time. The teachers of Crestwood Pines are learning that it is important to focus on a specific concept or topic and learn to develop expertise in this area instead of learning a little about many subjects. Mr. Wayne is excited to check in with the Technology Support Committee on a monthly basis to work through any gaps or issues that may be occurring and to support the use of technology to meet students' needs.

REFLECT AND APPLY ACTIVITIES

3.1. Based on the information that you have gathered in this chapter, your personal experience, and scholarly information about simulations in professional training, create a plan for utilizing a simulation assessment for new teachers. What type of scenario do you feel is best in assessing a new teacher's instruction in order to identify any strengths in teaching methods or gaps that need improvement? As an educational leader, what specific skills will you be looking to assess utilizing a simulation program such as Mursion?

3.2. Create a chart detailing the ways in which educators can utilize specific technology for professional development (see table 3.2).

Table 3.2   Technology for Professional Development

Technology Tool or Platform	Professional Development Use
EdPuzzle	• Interactive online lessons using video clips • Tracking learner progress
Podcasts	• Spark Creativity: ELA teachers • Truth for Teachers: practical tips for classroom • Chalk full of Life: emotional support

REFERENCES

Bandura, A. (1977). Self-efficacy: Toward a unifying theory of behavioral change. *Psychological Review, 84*, 191–215.

Bandura, A. (2001). Social cognitive theory: An agentic perspective. *Annual Review of Psychology, 52*, 1–26. doi: 10.1146/annurev.psych.52.1.1.

Boulton, M. (2014). Teachers' self-efficacy, perceived effectiveness beliefs, and reported use of cognitive-behavioral approaches to bullying among pupils: Effects of in-service training with the I DECIDE program. *Behavior Therapy, 45*(3), 328–43.

Brown, A. L., Lee, J., & Collins, D. (2015). Does student teaching matter? Investigating pre-service teachers' sense of efficacy and preparedness. *Teaching Education, 26*(1), 77–93. doi:10.1080/10476210.2014.957666.

Carpenter, J. P. & Krutka, D. G. (2014). How and why educators use *Twitter*: A survey of the field. *Journal of Research on Technology in Education, 46*(4), 414–34.

Chai, C. S., Koh, J. H. L., & Tsai, C. (2013). A review of technological pedagogical content knowledge. *Educational Technology & Society, 16*(2), 31–51.

Cox, S. & Graham, C. R. (2009). Diagramming TPACK in practice: Using and elaborated model of the TPACK framework to analyze and depict teacher knowledge. *TechTrends, 53*(5), 60–69.

Darling-Hammond, L. (2009). Teacher education and the American future. *Journal of Teacher Education, 61*, 35–47.

Felix, K. (2007, March–April). Free professional development podcasts. *Multimedia & Internet@Schools, 14*(2), 7.

Huza, A. (2017). How this school is successfully implementing video coaching, *Tech Decisions.* https://blog.edthena.com/2017/05/22/school-successfully-implementing-video-coaching-tech-decisions/.

Koh, J. H. L., Chai, C. S., & Lee, M. (2015). Technological pedagogical content knowledge (TPACK) for pedagogical improvement: Editorial for special issue on TPACK. *Asia-Pacific Education Researcher, 24*(3), 459–62. doi:10.1007/s40299-015-0241-6.

Lateef, F. (2010). Simulation-based learning: Just like the real thing. *Journal of Emergencies, Trauma and Shock, 3*(4), 348.

Mishra, P. & Koehler, M. J. (2006). Technological pedagogical content knowledge: A framework for teacher knowledge. *Teachers College Record, 108*(6), 1017–54.

Pamuk, S., Ergun, M., Cakir, R., Yilmaz, H. B., & Ayas, C. (2015). Exploring relationships among TPACK components and development of the TPACK instrument. *Education and Information Technologies, 20*(2), 241–63. doi:10.1007/s10639-013-9278-4.

Peterson, T. (2019). Technology starts with professional development and training. https://edtechmagazine.com/k12/article/2016/06/technology-starts-professional-development-and-training.

Ping, C., Schellings, G., & Beijaard, D. (2018). Teacher educators' professional learning: A literature review. *Teaching and Teacher Education, 75,* 93–104.

Seemiller, C. & Grace, M. (2017). Generation Z: Educating and engaging the next generation of students. *About Campus, 22*(3), 21–26.

Shatto, B. & Erwin, K. (2016). Moving on from millennials: Preparing for generation Z. *Journal of Continuing Education in Nursing, 47*(6), 253–54.

Shulman, L. (1986). Those who understand: Knowledge growth in teaching. *Educational Researcher, 15*(2), 4–14.

Virtual Reality Training Simulation Software by Mursion. (n.d.). https://www.mursion.com/

Williams, C. A. (2019). Nurse educators meet your new students: Generation Z. *Nurse Educator, 44*(2), 59–60. doi:10.1097/NNE.0000000000000637.

Wolpert-Gawron, H. (2018). The importance of choice in PD. https://www.edutopia.org/article/importance-choice-pd.

Woolfolk, A. E. & Hoy, W. K. (1990). Prospective teachers' sense of efficacy and beliefs about control. *Journal of Educational Psychology, 82,* 81–91. doi:10.1037/0022- 0663.82.1.81.

Zee, M. & Koomen, H. M. Y. (2016). Teacher self-efficacy and its effects on classroom processes, student academic adjustment, and teacher well-being: A synthesis of 40 years of research. *Review of Educational Research, 86*(4), 981–1015.

Chapter 4

Writing in a Digital Environment

Elisabeth Denisar

Gina Ciero arrived at her monthly English Leadership meeting with other department chairs and literacy coaches from her district. Scanning the agenda she saw that the focus of this month was statewide writing tests and best practice. This was not a new conversation in her school district. For years, they had been discussing how to "crack the testing code" to show solid test scores. Gina, like many other teacher leaders in her district, believes that teachers should focus on student learning, not on test scores.

The pressure to ensure that teachers' instructional practices translate into student achievement is a productive conversation that Gina's district and many others have year after year. However, this meeting added a new facet to the ongoing conversation surrounding writing performance on standardized tests. How do computer-based writing environments affect student performance on writing tests?

In the age of digital testing platforms, this question about digital literacy has become paramount for schools and districts. Is there a difference in the way students read and write digitally as compared to writing with pencil and paper? How do teachers and schools address digital writing when they do not have the technology available for every student to have digital access every day? Ultimately, how do school leaders and teachers know if the digital methods of teaching writing are empowering students and will translate to the skills needed for increased student performance on standardized tests?

WHERE TO BEGIN

After the meeting, Gina returned to her school ready to begin the conversation with her department and administrators surrounding maximizing student achievement on standardized writing tests in a digital environment. Her first step was to look at data from past writing tests. She knows that numbers are important. Starting with the data allows teams to look for ways that technology would influence the trends they see in student achievement, instruction, and student growth.

For teacher leaders, any time we infuse technology into our way of work, there will be change, and often rapid and repeated change. It is important to recognize that teachers will be at different places in their attitudes and aptitudes concerning technology. This can leave teachers feeling frustrated, afraid, and overwhelmed. According to Neal (2011), teachers' attitudes and fears about technology will shape the instructional application of digital tools and assessment. The starting point for instructional leaders is to welcome conversations from teachers who are at all places in their understanding and use of technology. The goal for these discussions is not to have all the answers but to drive the process that leads to our way of work.

THE WRITING PROCESS: THE FOUNDATION
FOR WRITING INSTRUCTION

Before Gina's department could consider how to integrate new ways of envisioning writing, they spent time identifying what they valued about writing instruction. One shared value emerged at the center of her department's work: the writing process. Much of the discussion centered around what does the writing process look like? Teachers of writing have been asking this question for many decades. In the *English Journal* in 1936, Grandy first described the idea of a "writing laboratory" (p. 374) where students worked with very different tasks, genres, and styles of writing. Students conferenced with each other, accessed resources, and received help from the teacher based on need (Grandy, 1936). Student writing requires time to process and revisit ideas. For students to grow in their writing abilities, students' need should drive instruction.

While the team decided that the concept of the writing process was at the core of the English classroom's way of work, they needed to should what was mean by the "writing process." They agreed that writing is not a linear, step-by-step approach or a formula, but rather a fluid movement in and out of cognitive processes. In an article entitled "All Children Can Write," Graves stated, "When children use a meaning-centered approach to writing, they compose in idiosyncratic ways. Each child's approach to composing is different from the next" (Graves, 1985, p. 36). What can be incredibly frustrating for many classroom observers is that there is no one-size-fits-all approach to teaching children how to write.

The following are common writing processes or stages that are taught explicitly in many classrooms:

• Prewriting/inquiry—the development and/or research of an idea, a hunch, a curiosity, or a question.
• Drafting—the organizing of language and images to craft ideas into a desired future format for publishing.
• Revising—the refinement of ideas and word choice by adding, clarifying, rearranging, or deleting.
• Editing/proofreading—the refinement of the working project for rules of language and conventions in preparation for publishing.
• Feedback/conferencing—the process of receiving input from others to improve the product or process.
• Publishing—the releasing of the product for the viewing of others.

Student writers grow when they examine their own writing choices. As they move in and out of the writing process, they not only learn about the topic of their writing, but they also learn about themselves. According to Anderson (2017), "As our students produce writing and, in that process, share themselves, they open themselves up to these same doubts. The moment they pick up a pen and scratch down their thoughts is the moment they become real writers" (p. 14). The role of the teacher is not to help students avoid these challenges but to help them work through these challenges. Students develop an ontology of not just how their topics, ideas, and perspectives fit into the world, but writers also discover their place within their writing.

When teachers and schools get to the heart of their instructional pedagogy, then the tough choices involving technology are made with student-centered understandings of what drives writing.

DOES DIGITAL WRITING MATTER?

Digital writing is important to not only our students' personal lives but their academic ones as well. We often hear that today's students are the digital natives, but our students need teachers who can guide them through the processes of effective written and digital composition. Teachers can capitalize on the tools with which students practice regularly in their digital lives to develop strategies that will translate into the academic writing.

Students who engage on social media platforms have experience not only in evaluating and analyzing meaning, perspective, and audience but students also use these environments to construct and respond through writing. On platforms such as Instagram or Snapchat, children are creators of hybrid texts that include both images and words for a specific audience. These writers receive immediate, authentic feedback on their project from their audience, both positive and negative. Some PK–12 and postsecondary schools have found value in social media-like platforms to provide English language learners, and all students, the opportunity to practice writing in low-threat, high-engagement environments with increased academic results by bridging academic performance opportunities with personal application (Freyn, 2017).

Another skill set that students practice in their digital life is indexing and paying contribution simultaneously—something that could never be accomplished without technology. With the use of hashtagging, tagging, and @ attributions, students create content on trending topics for targeted viewers. They tag others in photos, memes, and content to generate discussion and approval. They cite other users by using "@" attribution that not only gives credit but also invites others into their content. During the writing process, these skills are invaluable in inquiry as students are developing questions, researching keywords, and citing experts.

Hyler and Hicks (2017) described a way of crowdsourcing student learning of grammar by using hashtags with students on a classroom

Twitter page as they are observing how the writing rules of grammar are applied in their everyday lives. They observed that students often struggle with connecting syntax and grammar concepts to real writing. By using social media, students can develop these skills using their own voices and an authentic audience. For example, following a lesson on colons, students can expand their practice by incorporating the use of a colon in their writing. Student will use it in an informal setting and then use a hashtag that is preidentified with their teacher's name and school initials (e.g., #SmithORHS) to call out their usage. The teacher can then log students' usage by examining their content with the hashtag.

Additionally, students can also take note of how others use a skill by paying attribution. In that same lesson about colons, students can use the @ symbol to show where they found interesting use of colons. Perhaps when they are reposting song lyrics from a favorite musical artist, they can use an attribution to show the source and perhaps gain attention from their musical idol. Student would also include their classroom hashtag to crowdsource when someone makes use of colons. Teachers and classmates can use that hashtag not only to see original construction, but they also are now paying deliberate attention to writing that is part of their everyday lives. Many of the skills that students bring from their experience with digital content production benefit their academic writing performance. The challenge for schools is to translate these students' digital habits into classroom learning opportunities.

Another consideration for instructional leaders is not only where these opportunities intersect, but where they diverge. Are students' ideas fully developed in their digital worlds, or is the response just a knee-jerk reaction to a triggering topic? What constitutes a draft—a long blog post or a tweet? Is a response to a social media post considered feedback, or is it drafted content? (DeVoss et al., 2010).

What once seemed like blatant plagiarism is now a typical social media mashup of spoken word, beat loops, still and moving images, and original text. This shift in the world of online access has muddied what we consider common knowledge and what deserves to be credited (Bromley, 2010). While students in their online lives practice the process of writing regularly, the more significant challenge for teachers is that in digital environments, the writing process bends and blends what we have always held as true.

While a timed writing test on a computer may still be rooted in traditional essay-writing skill sets, the opportunity for prewriting, drafting, editing, and revision strategies found in digital writing has a direct impact on students' academic proficiency (Hutchison & Colwell, 2014). Gina's team must integrate what students bring to the writing table by blending rather than carve away students' digital lives outside of school from their academic writing development.

CAPITALIZING ON "OLD" MODES OF WRITING FOR DIGITAL WRITING

Gina's school, much like many others, does not have one computer for every child. Not all families have home devices for desktop publishing, nor do all families have access at home to the Internet. Teachers can only control what they can control. Therefore, Gina and her team benefit from an approach that focuses on the writing process, so they can prioritize how they use the limited digital access at her school. As a department, they decide they can use technology access to take students places they could not go with paper and pencil, but they need to consider the most effective way to use the limited number of digital devices.

The National Council of Teachers of English (NCTE) in *Beliefs for Integrating Technology into the English Language Arts Classroom* stated that "new technologies should be considered only when it is clear how they can enhance, expand, and/or deepen engaging and sound practices related to literacies instruction" (NCTE, 2018, para. 9). Many of our nondigital tools such as highlighting, notetaking, and graphic organizers can and should be incorporated even if technology is not limited. Learners do not have the use of a computer lab for the sheer purpose of taking notes to prepare for a class essay. However, there are new ways of working and exploring writing with the inclusion of sound, typeface, moving images, and social components that cannot be easily achieved without technology.

Schools do not need to view using technology in writing instruction as an either/or scenario that is in direct competition with other facets of writing instruction. Robust strategies that promote the learning process must transfer from one writing environment to another. Without the transference of new tools in a student's writing toolbox, it is not truly a strategy, but rather a fancy activity that perhaps increased students' interest. The focus on strategy and process-centered writing allows students to move in and out of writing environments empowered to take the tools from one situation to make choices about a different situation (Graham & Perin, 2007).

THE WRITING PROCESS: INNOVATION IS NOT THE ENEMY OF INSTRUCTION

Gina and her colleagues decided to focus on technology tools that would promote students' abilities to expand and develop as writers. It quickly became overwhelming to determine what was beneficial. Many textbook publishers offered fancy programs that graded student writing and generated computerized feedback. Some companies boasted about grammar improvement through online drills and video instruction. Others offered leveled language instruction that gamified word play to increase vocabulary. It would be easy to chase after every new shiny type of technology. This team needed to make effective choices about the best way to use their limited time and digital resources.

Technology is engaging for students' use during writing, but writing can be a very messy endeavor, and engagement does not always equal achievement. Wartella (2015) stated that learning happens "when children are 'minds-on'—that is, engaged in thinking, reflecting, and effortful mental activity" (p. 1). Just because students are tapping away at keyboards does not necessarily equal student growth. Teachers need to be mindful of learning outcomes, whether they are using technology or are going "old school" with paper and pencil.

It is important that teachers carefully weave digital writing experiences in district curriculum resources and state standards based on students' needs. Hicks (2009) reminded schools like Gina's that they should focus their efforts on real writing tasks by using technology to accomplish outcomes. Solid writing instruction infused with technology puts learners at the center. Technology should not become a frill, but rather a tool to take student writers to places they could not have traveled without it.

PREWRITING/INQUIRY

In collaboration with the librarian at Gina's school, teachers began establishing library guides from databases, which the school had available to assist students with inquiry using digital assets that could not be accessed through books and printed resources alone. Schools may want to explore digital concept mapping options such as *Prezi* (prezi.com) & *MindMUp* (mindmup.com), so students can organize text and notetaking into thinking clusters or ideas. Digital mapping allows students to establish direct links back to original sources while offering an infusion of video, images, and sounds that could never be present in paper-only concept maps.

Students can plan collaboratively in real time, either remotely or face-to-face, to explore ideas and incorporate multiple perspectives into their writing. Using digital resources, they can track their idea progression over time and record students' contributions. Teacher feedback can be provided to guide thinking asynchronously or in real time helping to enhance organization and the process of idea development (Dial & Vasquez, 2018). Using digital resources, this would look vastly different from a standard classroom where teachers run from group to group, trying to listen in on snippets of valuable conversations, hoping to get a glimpse of the collaborative environments.

DRAFTING

Gina's team next identified the use of digital drafting for longer pieces of real-world writing where students can metacognitively develop their writers' toolboxes. When students repeat skills from one environment to the next, they develop the ability to transfer skills to other pieces, which enhances success on timed-writing assessments (Hyler & Hicks, 2014).

Additionally, the skills students need to be successful constructing state standards composition are the very same skills required in digital environments where students create podcasts, videos, presentations, interactive flow charts, animated movies, and even video game narratives. Due to the multimodal facets of digital writing, many students perceive that they are engaging in higher-order thinking skills more often than they are during text-only writing (Yu, 2014).

Teachers must bring awareness to writing skills and model how digital environments directly translate to other writing environments, even timed-writing assessments, so students are empowered to access the strategies and skill sets they are using in other venues to create more effective written projects.

REVISING

For many of our students, they tend to take a "one-and-done" approach to pencil and paper writing projects. Revising in pencil and paper is quite laborious, and many classrooms try to teach to the test by having students repeatedly create semi-polished drafts that they never revise. This leaves students without an awareness of how and when to make changes in their writing.

Digital platforms enable students to internalize the revision process through analysis of their writing and tracking those changes over time. Students can use commenting features to note personal questions or areas that need improvement. The focus on recognizing why and how writers make decisions, coupled with tracking abilities in word processing software, helps student writers to consider how they are thinking and working through the refinement process (DeVoss et al., 2010).

PROOFREADING/EDITING

An editing concern in Gina's department centered around student dependence on word processing software to review convention errors. Put simply, students do not learn language conventions when they can have the computer to do the corrections for them. While this is a real concern, focusing on the process of editing can become a place of empowerment rather than enabling dependence on grammar and spell checkers.

Keeping a correction log is not new to classrooms. Many teachers hand back student papers with editorial notes for student correction. However, rather than having to wait for teacher feedback, computer word processing programs catch issues at the point of error. The benefit is that students pause, reflect, and correct their errors in the moment. This internalization is the same skill needed on timed-writing assessments. Having students keep learning logs of errors with consideration about why they made the error can help students learn from their mistakes in the moment rather than trying merely to let the computer fix them before turning in the assignments.

FEEDBACK/CONFERENCING

For many schools like Gina's, peer feedback and teacher conferencing are a large part of their way of work. This school regularly conducts conferences where students sit with the teacher one-on-one or in small groups to talk about their writing process during writing instruction. Digital writing can be multimodal and is not always linear in organization, so feedback is more complex.

Several companies offer tools for both digital and traditional text feedback, such as Flipgrid (flipgrid.com) and VoiceThread (voicethread.com). Students post work to be viewed. Peers and the teacher respond in written, oral, or video responses at the point needed for feedback. This is especially helpful for students with digital, nonlinear texts where feedback is essential for exploring new ways of thinking.

Moreover, video and oral response features offer students practice in giving quality responses. It is important to note that just because students are generating feedback through technology, they are not magically versed in how to provide quality commentary to peers. Technology does not supplant the role of the teacher. For students to craft meaningful feedback, teachers must model and guide students toward meaningful digital conversations (Hojeij & Hurley, 2017). Through technology learners can record and rerecord their suggestions until they are satisfied with their response. Responding allows all student writers to engage in the conversations about the production and craft of good writing. For English language learners or more timid students, this gives them a safe venue to be part of the classroom conversation while developing language, oral expression, and writing skills.

PUBLISHING

In digital writing, publishing takes on new meanings and encompasses new genres. Students are able to showcase more than just stories, poems, and essays. Digital publishing allows students to display very complex products such as interactive research, collaborative presentations, movies, podcasts, spoken word poetry, animated narratives, and so much more. For many, having students who are well versed in putting their lives in public view for everyone to see can often be terrifying. However, our students are already experienced users of social media. It is up to teachers to guide students through the vast landscape of digital exposure. Gold, Garcia, and Knutson (2019) described the five areas of concern that schools must address: presence, persistence, permeability, promiscuity, and power. Instructors are faced with many questions to answer. How do we guide students to anticipate which audiences to invite to the viewing table? How do we promote students' self-expression and yet guide responsible and ethical publishing of images, video, sound, and text that add to academic discourse without inflicting harm? Conversely, how do we help students in presenting their still unfamiliar authentic selves without provoking unintended consequences of their exploration? These concerns surrounding digital publishing must be addressed at both the school and district levels. Instructional leaders have a responsibility to their students and colleagues to determine how to navigate through the thrill and pitfalls of digital publishing.

Protocols and decisions about the platforms and the degree to which publishing opportunities are available are crucial choices. Organizations such as the NCTE have position statements that offer schools and districts guidance on how to make best practice decisions that promote learning and digital safety.

Some districts have chosen digital writing portfolios as blogs that follow the child from elementary school to graduation. Even emerging writers can post (with adult help) writing that not only highlights accomplishment but also serves as a way for young writers to tell their stories over time. Students begin to see themselves within the context of their own writing as they explore questions such as: "What is my style?" and "Where have I found success, growth, and change?" Moreover, while these are also components for traditional writing portfolios, digital portfolios expand audiences to not only the teacher and the student but also to peers, parents, future teachers, administrators, and other audiences that schools choose. This present and future audience is a catalyst for students to consider not only where they have been with their writing but also where they are headed (Hicks et al., 2007).

CONCLUSION

In Gina's school, they used the NCTE's position statement on Principles and Practices in Electronic Portfolios to focus their efforts on the outcomes that they wanted to achieve through portfolio development (NCTE, 2015). With a focus on digital production of writing, there are writing products that simply cannot be housed in a traditional portfolio. Digital portfolios offer students an opportunity to monitor their growth through considering many different writing environments that have value to them, rather than just focusing on essays. Most importantly, digital portfolios offer students limitless opportunities for revision, expansion, and innovation (Klages & Clark, 2009).

DeVoss et al. (2010) explained that "while digital writing tools will continue to have an impact on our classrooms and on our understanding of the writing process, by holding tight to core principles that have informed the writing process movement—and, indeed, informed the work of thousands of writing teachers over the past three decades—we can maintain a solid pedagogical base despite rapid changes in technology" (p. 60). Ultimately, Gina's team is making critical choices about ways technology fits into both student success on academic testing and also creates agile lifelong learners and writers in the digital world.

REFLECT AND APPLY ACTIVITIES

4.1. Consider what data your school would need to evaluate to determine students' writing needs. Create a data presentation to facilitate a conversation with your English department and other stakeholders about technology and writing needs.
4.2. Evaluate a technology tool you are not currently using that is available to increase student writing skills. Critique the tool using the criteria in table 4.1.

Table 4.1   Evaluation of a Technology Tool

Criteria	Characteristics
Description of the tool	
Standards/outcomes it addresses	
Other low or no tech options	
Cost-effectiveness	
Student accessibility inside of school	
Student accessibility outside of school	
Benefits of the tool	
Barriers or concerns about the tool	

REFERENCES

Anderson, J. (2017). Sharing our vulnerabilities as writers: Writing and revising even when you don't want to. *Voices from the Middle*, 25(2), 14–17.

Bromley, K. (2010). Picture a world without pens, pencils, and paper: The unanticipated future of reading and writing. *Journal of College Reading and Learning*, 41(1), 96–108. doi: 10.1080/10790195.2010.10850337.

DeVoss, D. N., Eidman-Aadahl, E., & Hicks, T. (2010). *Because digital writing matters: Improving student writing in online and multimedia environments.* Jossey-Bass.

Dial, J. S. & Vasquez, A. (2018). Google Drive: Facilitating collaboration and authentic community beyond the classroom. *Voices from the Middle*, 25(4), 24–28.

Freyn, A. L. (2017). Experimenting with Snapchat in a university EFL classroom. *Journal of Education and Practice*, 8(10), 35–37.

Gold, D., Garcia, M., & Knutson, A. V. (2019, Spring). Going public in an age of digital anxiety. *Composition Forum, 41.* http://compositionforum. com/issue/41/going-public.php.

Graham, S. & Perin, D. (2007). *Writing next: Effective strategies to improve writing of adolescents in middle and high schools.* Alliance for Excellent Education.

Grandy, A. (1936). A writing laboratory. *The English Journal, 25*(5), 372–76. doi:10.2307/805129.

Graves, D. H. (1985). All children can write. *Learning Disabilities Focus, 1*(1), 36–43.

Hicks, T. (2009). *The digital writing workshop.* Heinemann.

Hicks, T., Russo, A., Autrey, T., Gardner, R., Kabodian, A., & Edington, C. (2007). Rethinking the purposes and processes for designing digital portfolios: Digital portfolios can foster critical, creative, and reflective thinking for teachers (and their students, too). *Journal of Adolescent & Adult Literacy, 50*(6), 450–58.

Hojeij, Z. & Hurley, Z. (2017). The triple flip: Using technology for peer and self-editing of writing. *International Journal for the Scholarship of Teaching and Learning, 11*(1). doi: 10.20429/ijsotl.2017.110104.

Hutchison, A. C. & Colwell, J. (2014). The potential of digital technologies to support literacy instruction relevant to the Common Core State Standards. *Journal of Adolescent & Adult Literacy, 58*(2), 147–56. doi: 10.1002/jaal.335.

Hyler, J. & Hicks, T. (2014). *Create, compose, connect!: Reading, writing, and learning with digital tools.* Routledge.

Hyler, J. & Hicks, T. (2017). *From texting to teaching: Grammar instruction in a digital age.* Routledge.

Klages, M. A. & Clark, E. J. (2009). New worlds of errors and expectations: Basic writers and digital assumptions. *Journal of Basic Writing (CUNY), 28*(1), 32–49.

NCTE (2015, March 31). Principles and practices in electronic portfolios. https://ncte.org/statement/electronicportfolios/.

NCTE (2018, October 25). Beliefs for integrating technology into the English language arts classroom. https://ncte.org/statement/beliefs-technology-preparation-english-teachers/.

Wartella, E. (2015). Educational apps: What we do and do not know. *Psychological Science in the Public Interest, 16*(1), 1–2.

Yu, E. (2014). Let developmental students shine: Digital writing. *Research and Teaching in Developmental Education, 30*(2), 99–110.

Chapter 5

Digital Wellness in Our Schools

Brandy Pollicita

Mr. Taylor, a seventh-grade English Language arts teacher at Palm Middle School, scans the room checking out his first period class at the start of the school day. Madison and Alice are huddled together next to their desks appearing quite agitated, while Madison is looking at something on the phone. Enrique, who arrived early, has his headphones in but the music is so loud Mr. Taylor can hear it from the other side of the room. A trio of three girls is all standing around one desk using their phones to take pictures of their feet, while Marquis and Elijah are watching a YouTube video of their favorite gamer. Well, thought Mr. Taylor, I guess my students are just like every other middle school student. They are constantly on their digital devices until they are told to put them away.

Once the bell rings, Mr. Taylor reminds them to put their phones away and so begins the ritual of some students placing them in backpacks and pockets, while others hide them under their leg or simply inside their shirt or pants. This seems like a pointless game, Mr. Taylor thinks, and I am the only one who loses. They are constantly finding new places to hide their cell phones, rather than putting them away.

Mr. Taylor divides the class into groups and hands each student a worksheet to be completed and submitted by the end of the class period. Once the groups begin the activity, Mr. Taylor walks around to ensure that everyone understands the assignment and is actively participating. Within five minutes, Madison's group is laughing loudly while passing a phone around the group. The girls are asked to put the phone away and refocus on the activity but within minutes Madison has the phone back in her hands. Mr. Taylor walks over and takes the phone from Madison and tells her she can pick it up at the office at the end of the day. One of the other girls starts crying and Madison seems visibly shaken by losing the cell phone and asks to go see Ms. Wang, the school counselor.

"Madison, what is going on?" inquired Ms. Wang.

"You won't believe it! It's just not fair," complained Madison. "My parents 'digitally grounded' me and I don't know when I will get my cell phone back. I borrowed Jessica's phone to check my social media account and then Mr. Taylor took Jessica's phone away. Now, Jessica is mad at me for losing her phone. Without my phone I can't socialize with any of my friends or even talk to my boyfriend!" she complained. Ms. Wang tried to discuss the whole situation with Madison, but she did not make a lot of progress.

After sending Madison back to class, Ms. Wang proceeds to her weekly meeting with Ms. Martin, the principal, where they have been discussing the problem of students using their mobile devices during class. This problem just seems to keep coming up. The level of distraction and disruption phones are causing is a constant problem. Students are noncompliant and teachers are not consistently enforcing the no cell phone policy. The district has conducted training with teachers and staff, but this does not seem to be addressing the problem. Perhaps students aren't aware of their behavior or maybe they are addicted. Ms. Wang has seen many students in her office who seem tired, anxious, and affected by "digital drama" as a result of poor choices while communicating with their phone.

Ms. Martin muses, "I think there are some questions we need to answer. Maybe you can investigate this for me. What does the research say about how much phone use is detrimental to student development? Is it how they are using their devices that is the problem? Are the phones the root of student underachievement? If so, how have other schools worked to alleviate the problem? Can you check those questions out and get back to me by our meeting next week? Maybe when we have more answers we can come up with a credible solution."

INTRODUCTION

June 29, 2007, is when a "new normal" began with the release of the first iPhone. This invention would impact how we communicate, what we communicate, and even when we communicate. It would build relationships with people around the globe yet spawn mayhem with our neighbors. It would allow for multitasking at the next level, which has been transformed into hours of extended screen time. Adults and children began a love/hate relationship with a device that could provide access to the world and give the world access to them. Unfortunately, on that fatefully day in 2007 we lacked the foresight to understand that these devices would become so pervasive in our culture that even young children would have their own mobile phones. Eighty-nine percent of middle school and high school adolescents own a personal mobile device (Rideout & Robb, 2018). Even though the idea of protecting the health and safety of our developing youth is embedded in our society, young children are handed a device that oftentimes puts their well-being at risk.

The research findings on youth technology usage vary as a result of the perpetual introduction of new devices and apps. Current research reported that youths spend an average of nine hours a day on a digital device (Rideout & Robb, 2018); however, the specific type of devices and the programs they are using are continually evolving and changing. Frequently, by the time recommendations related to a specific device or platform are published, the device or program is obsolete. Nonetheless, a review of current research on youth and digital devices can serve to determine overall trends and the positive and negative effects. Particularly, how these devices and their content affect youths' well-being during development and specifically their impact in the learning environment is an important consideration. It would benefit educators to have a broad understanding of how the use of digital devices affects students' academic achievement and attendance.

Wellness, as a multidimensional model of health and well-being, is an important consideration, especially during the formative years. Research has examined the effects technology has on the various components of youth development, along with providing recommendations for ensuring healthy development. Promising strategies for preventing and resolving digital wellness concerns are an important consideration.

YOUTH DIGITAL LANDSCAPE

Educators have harnessed the availability of personal digital devices by integrating educational websites and apps into classroom activities. Unfortunately, the mere presence of personal mobile devices has provided an opportunity for digital disruptions in class or for allowing outside "digital drama" to spill over into the learning environment. Besides distractions to the learning environment, it has become apparent that technology usage may be responsible for adverse health-related effects that impede school performance.

Digital devices are not used in the same way by all youths. It is relevant to distinguish the types of digital devices and typology of programs, as preferences differ between genders and across age groups. The types of digital devices that youth may operate include traditional nonmobile devices such as televisions, PCs, and gaming consoles; semimobile devices such as laptops and iPads/tablets; and mobile handheld devices like smartphones and handheld gaming devices. Young people choose one device over another based on what they can accomplish with it. Recently, as interest in social media has grown, adolescents are drawn to handheld devices. According to the Lexico Dictionary (n.d.), social media is defined as "websites and applications that enable users to create and share content or to participate in social networking." Under this umbrella of social media are several subcategories, or platforms, including social networking, media sharing, and discussion forums to name a few.

Younger students, from birth to eight-year-olds, use television to watch programs and videos more often than they use mobile devices (fifty-eight minutes as compared to forty-eight minutes); however, the current usage of mobile devices is four times what it was four years ago (Rideout, 2017). Children between the ages of five and eight years of age spend approximately three hours a day on screen time, with a third of that time occurring on a handheld device to play games, watch videos, read books, and access apps (Rideout, 2017). As a result, parents report being concerned about the amount of screen time and its content, and so they frequently look to schools for advice and recommendations on how to handle this issue (Rideout, 2017). The American Academy of Pediatricians (AAP) recommends no more than one hour of screen time for two- to five-year-olds and for those over six years of age they recommend placing consistent limits on the time using media and the types of media to ensure that usage does not interfere with the recommended amount of sleep, physical activity, and other behaviors essential to health (AAP, 2016).

Tweens, ages eight to twelve years of age, average just under five hours of screen media usage a day with one to two hours being spent on television watching on such time-shifted programming as Netflix (Rideout & Robb, 2019). Fifty-six percent of these youth report watching online videos "every day" and over 50 percent of the age group have a smartphone by the age of eleven (Rideout & Robb, 2019). Forty-one percent of their screen time is spent on a mobile device with daily screen time at fifty-six minutes for tablets, forty-eight minutes on a smartphone, and thirty minutes on computers (Rideout, 2015). This age group uses these devices for a multitude of purposes but there are differences in usage between genders. Rideout (2015) determined that male tweens were predominantly interested in video games (68 percent). Alternatively, female tweens seemed to engage more in social networking (70 percent), reading (57 percent), and video viewing (57 percent). Mobile gaming, which encompasses games played on handheld devices, was reported as equally enjoyable for boys and girls (Rideout, 2015).

Adolescence seems to be the time when mobile device use drastically increases and morphs. Teens, age thirteen to seventeen years of age, report screen time nearly nine hours a day with more than six of those hours dedicated to screen media (Rideout, 2015). Forty percent of this group indicated that they preferred time-shifted programs (Rideout & Robb, 2019). Rideout and Robb (2018) determined that nearly 90 percent of students own a smartphone by the time they reach this milestone and 70 percent connected with social media multiple times a day. Sixty-nine percent of this group also self-reported watching online videos every day (Rideout & Robb, 2019). Teens indicated that they preferred to communicate with friends through their devices rather than face-to-face (Rideout & Robb, 2018). According to the latest Pew Research Survey (Anderson & Jiang, 2018), 45 percent of adolescents, age thirteen to seventeen years of age, are online on a nearly constant basis as compared to only 24 percent of this age group in 2014–2015. Adolescents reported "hardly ever" or "never" silencing or putting away their devices when doing homework (37 percent) or going to sleep (26 percent) (Rideout & Robb, 2018). Teens reported primarily engaging with social media platforms such as YouTube (85 percent), Instagram (72 percent), and Snapchat (69 percent) but also revealed they were concerned about their peer groups' excessive use of social media (Anderson and Jiang, 2018). Teen boys spend approximately fifty-six minutes a day playing video games and 27 percent reported it as their favorite media activity, while teen girls ranked listening to music as their preferred media activity (37%) but also reported spending approximately one hour and thirty-two minutes on social media (Rideout, 2015). With so many options in devices and platforms, choices diversify across other demographics.

Digital device trends have mainly highlighted variance between gender and across age groups, but preliminary findings suggest income levels, parent education, and race/ethnicity may also factor into usage trends. Children, ages from birth to eight years of age, from lower-income homes spend more than double the amount of screen time each day as compared to children from higher-income homes (three hours twenty-nine minutes vs. one hour fifty minutes) (Rideout, 2017). Tweens and teens from lower-income families and homes with lower levels of parent education spend more time connecting with media than those from higher-income homes, regardless of the device. Racial differences were also evident. Black teens recorded the most amount of time using media at approximately 11 hours a day as compared to Hispanics (eight hours fifty-one minutes) and whites (eight hours twenty-seven minutes) (Rideout, 2015). Another interesting discovery was a divergence in parental concern over content with whites least concerned (28 percent), followed by African Americans (38 percent), and followed by Hispanic/Latinos (54 percent) (Rideout, 2017). It is not surprising that with the escalation of personal device use across all demographics, educators have become more aware and concerned about the development and well-being of students. Ergo, speculating if the standard model of wellness is still applicable and that perhaps including new dimensions or reconfiguring assessments of wellness may need to be updated. A brief overview of the predominant wellness models used in research and practice and their application to youth reveal many needed modifications in this digital world.

WELLNESS AS A MODEL FOR DIGITAL INTERVENTION

In 1976, the Six Dimensions of Wellness model was created by Bill Hettler to illustrate the areas that impact overall health and well-being. The goal of this model was to establish a guideline for living a better existence by actively seeking improvement in each of the six different dimensions. These original dimensions included intellectual, emotional, social, spiritual, occupational, and physical (Hettler, 1976) and are the cornerstone for many other wellness models. Example behaviors can be found in table 5.1.

As research was conducted on factors that impact well-being, additional wellness models were introduced and suggested for specific cohorts. Several models of wellness targeting youth have been proposed, since these youngsters are still developing physically and

Table 5.1   Examples of Dimensions of Wellness

Dimension	Example Behaviors
Physical	• Stay active • Develop adequate nutrition • Practice appropriate substance intake (alcohol and drugs) • Seek medical attention when necessary • Engage in disease prevention behaviors
Emotional	• Develop emotional awareness • Engage in appropriate expression • Manage emotions • Demonstrate responsibility
Social	• Interacting with others • Develop a sense of community • Act socially responsible • Engage in advocacy
Intellectual	• Seek growth through inquiry • Develop lifelong learning • Pursue challenges
Occupational	• Perform optimally • Create a work ethic to reflect values and interests • Enjoy the profession • Be proactive in occupational duties
Spiritual	• Develop a sense of values and beliefs • Search for meaning and purpose • Pursue harmony and peace

mentally. One adolescent wellness model was designed specifically so that nurses could better understand the relationship between wellness and the developmental stages of an adolescent's life (Spurr et al., 2012). The study explored areas of wellness for adolescents, ages sixteen to twenty years of age, and found the most significant contributions to their perception of wellness included physical, psychological, spiritual, and social components. The U.S. Department of Health and Human services endorses an eight-dimension model for youth and young adults adding financial and environmental wellness to Hettler's six-dimension model (Martin et al., 2016).

Common Sense, a nonprofit organization aimed at aiding youth to excel in a world of technology, frequently surveys youth on their technology use and its perceived effects. They use a model of wellness that focuses on the social and emotional components called the Social-Emotional Well-Being (SEWB) scale. This eleven-item scale includes assessments of youth happiness, depression, loneliness, confidence, self-esteem, and parental relations within their digital world, along with their perceptions of how social media impacts feelings of depression, anxiety, popularity, loneliness, and confidence (Rideout & Robb, 2018). While there is no single prevailing model for youth wellness, experts agree it is a multidimensional consideration as many developing elements are affected by the use of digital devices. The impacts of both positive and negative digital device usage on youth physical health, emotional well-being, productivity (school and individual), relationships and communication, character and identity, and personal safety have been researched.

TECH EFFECTS ON YOUTH WELLNESS: "EXPECTATION VERSUS REALITY"

As previously discussed, traditional adult wellness models use the term "physical wellness"; however, a model sufficient for youth would need to account for ongoing development and the stages of maturation. For example, research determined that adults who use their mobile phones in bed before falling asleep have poorer quality sleep and higher rates of fatigue (Exelmans & Van den Bulck, 2016). The assumption is that the phone correlated to this adverse effect, but we cannot infer the same relationship for youth.

Development impacts many areas of wellness and so rather than replicating adult studies, it is best to perform research on youth. This area of research, although relatively new, has revealed areas of youth wellness that are being affected by digital devices.

Physical Health

According to the American Sleep Academy, six- to twelve-year-olds should acquire greater than nine hours of sleep a night (nine to twelve hours) while teens, ages thirteen to eighteen, need at least eight hours of sleep (eight to ten hours) (Paruthi et al., 2016). Unfortunately, technology has been linked to a shortage of youth sleep. The Center for Disease Control (CDC) found that teens who spent more than three hours a day on any electronic device were 28 percent more likely to get less than seven hours of sleep (CDC, 2015) and Kimball and Cohen (2019) found a link between youth excessive Internet usage and sleep disturbances. Emotional investments in social media can result in reduced sleep quality, as well (Woods & Scott, 2016). A reduction in the length of sleep time was found with youths' increased access to devices at nighttime (Chahal et al., 2013), particularly after 9:00 p.m. (Falbe et al., 2015). Grover and colleagues (2016) found adolescents who used digital devices after bedtime exhibited significantly more sleepiness and poorer academic accomplishments.

Technology usage has been detrimental in other areas of youth physical development and physical activity. An increased occurrence of risk factors associated with cardiovascular disease has been discovered in children. A survey of youth found that three or more hours of screen time was associated with obesity (Nightingale et al., 2017) and each daily hour of screen time was linked to a rise in diastolic blood pressure over seven years (Gopinath et al., 2014). The overuse of technology has led to the creation of new vision ailments in both adults and children. Computer vision syndrome (CVS), also called digital eye strain, is a collection of symptoms related to the overuse or misuse of technology. Symptoms include eyestrain, tired eyes, irritation, red vision, and blurred vision (American Optometric Association, 2020). The American Academy of Ophthalmology (2018) stated there is a strong indication that the increased use of digital devices is resulting in higher numbers of myopia, or nearsightedness, in youth. New orthopedic injuries such as ninten-donitis, a repetitive strain injury from gaming, have been identified in adolescents (Macgregor, 2000). Because of time spent on digital devices, tweens and teens are also not engaging in the recommended amount of daily physical activity (Rideout, 2015). These are just a few of the physical ailments youth may develop, but more research has gained educators' attention when it comes to the psychosocial impacts of digital devices.

Emotional Well-Being

To assess adolescent feelings, relating to emotional well-being, a combination of paradigms was used to design a survey tool. The SEWB scale is comprised of questions that measure an adolescent's self-perception of happiness, depression, loneliness, confidence, self-esteem, and parental relations. This survey was administered in 2018 to thirteen- to seventeen-year-old adolescents to measure their self-perceptions concerning social media (Rideout & Robb, 2018). The survey was able to differentiate those with lower self-perceptions as a result of social media from those that had higher, or more positive, views. Results indicated that 46 percent of those with low SEWB responded that social media is "extremely" or "very" important in their lives and also experienced more negative responses on social media including 35 percent reported being cyberbullied (Rideout & Robb, 2018). Investigators concluded that social media appeared to play a more significant role in the lives of those on the lower end of the SEWB scale.

Some interesting results have been found with social media use in unique groups of adolescents. Adolescents, fourteen to twenty-two years of age, who self-reported moderate to severe depressive symp-toms, indicated that social media made them feel less alone, provided a place to gain inspiration, and provided a medium for creative self-expression (Rideout & Fox, 2018). Unfortunately, about one-third (32%) reported that after viewing social media they felt others were "doing better than them." It should be noted that previous research had suggested that the way adolescents use social media, either pas-sive (scrolling with no interaction) or active (commenting), would correlate with depression, but that was not substantiated in this study. Self-reported frequency of digital drama, such as being "trolled" (someone instigating drama with them), "stalking" someone on social media (checking people out online without them knowing), and deleting a social media account after a personal conflict were all higher for those with depressive symptoms (Rideout & Fox, 2018). There has also been research that examined if digital devices were creating the opposite problems, such as excessive energy or attention deficit.

In 1997 the first national survey of parent-reported ADHD behaviors was collected, and since then the diagnosis numbers continue to grow (CDC, 2020). Researchers, intrigued with identifying the basis for this surge, have looked to see if technology has resulted in the booming ADHD diagnoses. Weiss et al. (2011) studied the ADHD-like behaviors in youth and speculated that the symptoms were not an indication of ADHD but that the high-stimulation video game content may result in behaviors that mimic the disorder. Many parents of youth with ADHD report their child almost seems addicted to their digital devices. The etymology of the word "addiction" goes back many centuries, and it was predominantly used when referring to behaviors associated with substance misuse. However, the term "well-being" is not clearly defined by the medical community.

This traditional focus on substance misuse has not deterred researchers from investigating "Internet addiction," "gaming addiction," or "social media addiction" under the guise of a "disorder." Both the American Psychological Association (APA) and the World Health Organization (WHO) have recognized digital device disorders. APA DSM-V includes Internet gaming disorder (IGD) after research revealed similarities in the symptoms of habitual gamers and substance users including comparable brain scans. WHO's International Classification of Diseases (ICD-11), analogous to the DSM-V, recently recognized gaming disorder as a diagnosis. While these major health and professional organizations seem to be connecting overuse of video games with negative impacts, the nature of the relationship between a developing child and video games, or any digital device, may be quite different.

Meerkerk and colleagues (2009) posit that individuals may be addicted "on the Internet" rather than "to the Internet"; this refers to the addiction to the activity (social networking, viewing videos, etc.) rather than to the broader Internet itself. Pornography addiction in youth is an area of interest for researchers with one technology security company reporting 10 percent of visitors to pornography sites are under the age of ten years (Muresan, 2016). Studies on these variables will continue but designs may be flawed if researchers do not consider that devices and platforms are intentionally designed to be used compulsively with easy access, autoplay, and endless feeds. Before labeling a child, many experts recommend using the term "problematic Internet use," or PIU, when discussing the ill effects technology has on a child's well-being. Several new technical mental illnesses have been propositioned including "nomophobia," anxiety over not having one's phone, and "phantom vibration syndrome," a tactile hallucination whereby you feel your phone vibrate when it does not. These terms, while somewhat witty, are not medical terms and warrant more research before using them to identify youths' behavior. Regardless of labels, educators should be mindful of the effects overuse may have in the school setting both emotionally and academically.

Productivity

Kindt and colleagues (2019) examined a correlation between Internet use disorder (IUD) and school-relevant factors such as attendance, grades, social behavior at school, procrastination, and learning behavior. The participants were those at a higher risk for compulsive Internet use and results indicated that IUD symptoms were a predictor of procrastination, time spent online, and gaming at the individual level, and social behavior predicted symptoms of IUD at the school level.

Multitasking has long been touted as a method to save time, yet research determined that it often hinders productivity because the rate of work slows down because of having to maintain multiple trains of thought (Felt & Robb, 2016). Over two decades ago, a technology expert, Linda Stone, labeled this continuous division of attention as "continuous partial attention" to describe the effect multitasking via digital devices was having on other facets of our world. Even so, youth have self-reported multitasking "often" while doing homework while listening to music (76 percent), texting (60 percent), and interacting with social media (50 percent) (Rideout, 2015). Teens believe listening to music while doing homework helps (50 percent) and feel it neither helps nor hurts their homework performance to watch TV (63 percent), social network (55 percent), or sending text messages (64 percent) while working (Rideout, 2015). In the same report, tweens reported they do not believe operating a digital device helps but they do not feel it is detrimental to completing homework efficiently. While research is clear that multitasking negatively impacts productivity by requiring re-attention to a task, more research is needed to analyze how devices or platforms, such as time-shifted mediums, impact productivity. Adolescents are not aware of the detriment digital devices have on productivity, but they do report how these devices impact their relationships and social communication.

Relationships and Communication

Eighty-one percent of adolescents feel social media allows them to feel more connected with friends' lives, and 68 percent feel it allows others to support them during tough times (Anderson & Jiang, 2018). Teens are constantly adopting new modes of interacting but social networking and user-generated content (UGC) are the most popular subcategories of social media. Social networking was a concept long before the introduction of technological devices; however, the primary method for social networking has become digital. Youth still seek peer approval whether face-to-face or through social networking. However, the digital domain has changed the way this feedback is received because of an increase in anonymous feedback platforms used through social networking sites. Feedback and approval have also been quantified with the use of these sites through tracking "likes" and "views." The problem with these forums is that they allow for online social cruelty, such as cyberbullying or online public condemnation, which can be detrimental especially during the crucial stage of social development.

Social capital in the digital domain is a product of an individual's impact on a particular subculture that the individual identifies with and from which he seeks acceptance. UGC platforms allow youth to cultivate their social capital. Currently, the most popular sites allow for the creation of memes or short videos that support a movement, stance, or reflect current popular culture. Examples of trendy UGC platforms include Instagram (teens), TikTok (tweens), and Roblox (youth). As the content they produce is "viewed," "liked," or recreated, their social capital increases.

Utilizing devices while tending to other tasks reduces productivity, but this behavior can also harm the development of communication skills. Fifty-four percent of teens self-reported that they focus on their devices even when they are with other people (Rideout & Robb, 2018). A recent study reported that teens stated that they prefer communicating with friends via text (35 percent) rather than face-to-face (32 percent). These results may indicate that digital devices are eroding social communication skills, or it could be an indicator that this generation has decided on an alternative platform that is just as effective for bonding with friends and family. It also could be an indicator that youth are "overscheduled" starting at a very young age and by their adolescents are completely overextended. Perhaps digital devices are not a distraction but allow for the healthy engagement with society. Teen development is dependent on socializing, or networking, with their peers. It allows for peer guidance, feedback, and support at a time when they are exploring their identity and actively seeking independence from their caregivers.

Character and Identity

The development of one's identity is a journey that begins in early adolescence, as young people seek independence yet acceptance into a community. As young adolescents are experiencing physical changes and sexual maturation, new behaviors are tested to explore their "coming of age." This normal stage of development is also usually marked with the onset of risky behaviors that coincides with physiological and sexual changes. In this digital age, youth are inundated with images and videos depicting ideals that are usually misinterpreted as the norm. PIU, previously mentioned, may include behaviors that are a product of this goal to conform to the idealized norm. Examples include posting inappropriate images or videos that seem ephemeral to the youth, which in actuality are permanent. This Internet history, of sorts, is what becomes an individual's digital footprint, or more recently referred to as a digital tattoo.

Digital tattoos, like tattoos on skin, are permanent and even when efforts are made to remove them, it is a massive undertaking that may not be successful. Educating youth on the effects these digital tattoos can have on their future is not an easy process. It is nearly impossible for a developing child to understand the assumption that may be inferred by future employers, teachers, friends, and partners. The most recent conclusions, though, are that digital tattoos are no longer a solo project. Tweens and teens allow images and videos to be taken and posted by others continually. Oftentimes, these individuals are acquaintances but with the increase in "virtual friends," people may interact solely online usually from distant origins; consequently, inappropriate chats or snaps may also resurface. Requests for inappropriate images or receiving unsolicited images have increased with the hypersexualized culture online. A way to combat this is to have youth actively build a positive social identity that can be a source of pride. One suggestion is to construct a space where they can establish a positive voice, dialogue, and civic engagement (Kahne et al., 2015) especially when 27 percent of teens feel social media is "extremely" or "very" important for expressing themselves creatively (Rideout & Robb, 2018). Building a positive image is something youth will take pride in and, when done safely, can maintain privacy while building social capital.

Personal Safety

Privacy and security are a mainstay in digital citizenship models. These models integrate best practices to ensure youth are being balanced and safe when using technology. Safety online is crucial for the well-being of our developing children as they may still lack adequate means for assessing risk. As mentioned previously, sexual content has become a part of sexual exploration, but the age at which this begins can affect development and put a child at risk. Jiminy, a parenting app used to keep a child's phone safe, reviewed 54 million text messages and found alarming results. They discovered by age thirteen, 37 percent of youth have encountered sexting, defined as risqué games, references to sexual activity, sending "nude" pictures or videos, and livestreaming sexual activities (Jiminy, 2019). They also reported by age eight 10 percent of youth have participated in sexting with the peak at age fourteen (41 percent) and that girls contribute more than boys except at age fourteen when 43 percent of boys engage in the behavior. The risk associated with this behavior is not just a negative digital tattoo but usually encourages active participation by the child, which could be with someone they know or an unknown person they met online (Jiminy, 2019).

The legalities around possessing and producing images and videos are a safety concern for minors. The government can prosecute an adult for the production, distribution, reception, and possession of child pornography (which could be a sexted image of a minor). Sexting, in many states, is differentiated from child pornography especially when the sexting occurs between two minors. Students should be made aware of their state's sexting laws in all areas of prosecution (mentioned above for adults) as some states will issue a citation and others will prosecute as a felony.

School administrators have recognized, for some time, digital effects on their students. Many have implemented programs to assist students' navigation of the digital world to reduce the abovementioned consequences. Digital citizenship was one of the first terms coined to address how to "behave" in the digital world decades ago but only recently has infiltrated the school setting.

DIGITAL WELLNESS ROOTS AND RECOMMENDATIONS

Digital citizenship is a term that was coined by political scientist Karen Mossberger (2008), when, along with her colleagues, she wrote the book *Digital Citizenship: The Internet, Society, and Participation*. Soon this paradigm was adopted and modified to assist educators in the K–12 setting. One initial model was outlined in the text *Digital Citizenship in Schools*, which inspired the responsibilities of educators and students utilizing digital tools both in and outside of the classroom (Ribble & Bailey, 2007). The original curriculum consisted of nine elements: Digital Access is full electronic participation in society; Digital Commerce refers to the electronic buying and selling of goods; Digital Communication is the electronic exchange of information; Digital Literacy includes teaching and learning about technology and the use of technology; Digital etiquette is the electronic standards of conduct or procedure; Digital Law encompasses the electronic responsibility for actions and deeds; Digital Rights and Responsibilities are the requirements and freedoms extended to everyone in a digital world; Digital Health and Wellness is the physical and psychological well-being in a digital technology world; and Digital Security refers to the electronic precautions to guarantee safety (Ribble & Bailey, 2007).

An additional text *Digital Citizenship in Action: Empowering Students to Engage in Online Communities*, authored by Kristen Mattson (2017), highlighted the need for participatory citizenship by students and targeted educators to incorporate a digital citizenship curriculum. The text discouraged the practice of schools banning digital handheld devices altogether and instead encouraged students to actively engage with their devices. This text stressed the importance of educators mentoring students on digital platforms such as social networking sites. The International Society for Technology in Education (ISTE), an organization that supports technology in the classroom, has also set criteria around the use of technology. They regularly publish Standards for Students, Standards for Educators, and Standards for Administrators. Digital citizenship and balance are woven across all of the standards indicating the significance the organization places on digital wellness. ISTE has also joined forces to create a coalition tasked with redefining digital citizenship. This coalition, Digital Citizenship Commitment (DigCitCommit), aims to engage educators in the sharing of best practices and provide them with the tools to teach the revised digital citizenship and well-being model.

The mission of DigCitCommit (https://digcitcommit.org/) includes five target areas: Inclusive Citizenship, which involves being open to multiple viewpoints and respectful and empathetic to other online; Informed Citizenship, which encourages evaluating the accuracy and validity of digital media; Engaged Students stresses participation in civic engagement to solve problems and do good; Balanced Use focuses on prioritizing time and activities on and offline; and Alert Citizenship refers to being safe and creating safe space. Different digital citizenship models include a variety of factors but using digital devices in a healthy way to promote overall balance and wellness is a constant in all versions. Digital wellness is not a new term but addressing healthy digital use in the school curriculum is new territory for some school districts, especially with the evolving topics that characterize youth wellness in the digital realm.

In the school setting it is common practice to facilitate wellness campaigns to increase awareness in a specific area of contention, and to ultimately affect behavior positively. Many schools have programs dedicated to decreasing substance misuse, improving mental health, or increasing personal safety. These programs, whether intentional or not, are designed with a wellness model approach. For example, most schools enforce a tardy policy that will encourage professionalism in future occupational endeavors. That is just one example of how the school is an ideal setting to support the development of students. With the growing recommendations from prominent youth-focused health organizations on digital wellness, the adoption of these policies will significantly serve students and parents.

The foremost authority on healthy media habits for youth is Common Sense, a nonprofit organization providing insight and guidance for various forms of media. In 2010, Common Sense Education collaborated with Project Zero at the Harvard School of Education to create a new digital citizenship curriculum and it quickly became the dominant resource for educators. The curriculum covered the following eight components: Privacy and Security for students using digital devices; Self-image and Identity with a focus on the youth's "digital identity"; Relationships and Communication allowing students to reflect on positive interpersonal skills; Cyberbullying and Digital Drama exploring roles people and actions play online; Digital Footprint and Reputation learning how to protect and respect ourselves and others' privacy; Creative Credit and Copyright reflecting on responsibilities to creators of content online; Information Literacy provides strategies for identifying valid information online; and Internet Safety offering a framework for interacting with others near and far online.

In 2019, Common Sense Education unveiled a new model to offer a more relevant, targeted, and age-appropriate curriculum. This new curriculum condensed eight components to six including Privacy and Security, which is being aware of everyone's privacy; Digital Footprint and Identity explores defining who we are online; Media Balance and Well-Being including finding balance in our digital lives; Relationships and Communication understanding the power of our words and actions online; Cyberbullying, Digital Drama, and Hate Speech reflecting on digital kindness; and News and Media Literacy creating critical thinkers and creators. The curriculum is provided for each grade so that each grade has six lesson plans mirroring the six topics (James et al., 2019). Many schools have implemented elements of the Digital Citizenship Curriculum and have found it to be an important addition to their curriculum.

A survey of 16,906 education professionals was conducted by Schoology to provide a comprehensive analysis of the digital learning environment and 32.2 percent of the professionals reported their school required students to complete a digital citizenship program (Schoology, 2020). The participants also reported that the top areas of concern within digital citizenship were Internet safety (84.3 percent), cyberbullying (80.7 percent), privacy, and security (66.4 percent). The most interesting finding was that the majority of teachers (56 percent) felt social media was a problem at their school, while only 49 percent of administrators reported it was a problem (Schoology, 2020). This could be an indication of a disconnect between administrators and the students or teachers. Teachers have more interactions with students, although administrators are usually the initiators of a digital wellness campaign.

Professionals within the school system who also can pursue a digital wellness initiative are school counselors and educational technology officers. School counselors should play an essential role in any improvement practices and are usually the driving force behind programs that impact achievement, attendance, and behavior. A digital wellness program could be an avenue for school counselors to engage all students, educators, and administrators through the creation of a committee. The educational technology staff could help provide appropriate guidance for both students and staff in and outside of school.

Hilliard City Schools, a suburban school district in Columbus, Ohio, has built a prominent digital wellness program led by their educational technology staff. A Digital Wellness Month was the initial format, which concentrated on these four areas: Digital Wellness (how to be healthy while using technology), Digital Citizenship (responsible and honest online activity), Online Etiquette (communicating with kindness and ethical behavior online), and Online Safety (how to stay safe and protect private information online). The program made sure to include teachers, coaches, and parents with both in-school and out-of-school assignments. Although this campaign focused on digital wellness for one month, other possible avenues school could explore would include weekly topics throughout the year, daily announcements, student-created Public Service Announcements (PSAs), utilization of apps that encourage students to unplug at school, parent night, blogs, and more. The options are unlimited, but it is important to attempt to recruit as many stakeholders as possible to further the impact on a child's digital life.

REFLECT AND APPLY ACTIVITIES

5.1. Talk to the leadership in your setting and investigate the current digital policies in place to protect your learners in the digital environment. How do these align with the specific procedures and policies discussed in this chapter? Identify any additional policies and procedures that should be added to your current safeguards.

5.2. Create a pamphlet for your learners or your learners' parents that explains the policies and procedures that would be appropriate for the age group with which you work.

REFERENCES

American Academy of Ophthalmology. (2018). *Is too much screen time harming children's vision.* https://www.aao.org/newsroom/news-releases/detail/is-too-much-screen-time-harming-childrens-vision.

American Optometric Association. (2020). *Computer vision syndrome.* https://www.aoa.org/patients-and-public/caring-for-your-vision/protecting-your-vision/computer-vision-syndrome.

Anderson, M. & Jiang, J. (2018, November 28). *Teens' social media habits and experiences.* Pew Research Center. https://www.pewresearch.org/internet/2018/11/28/teens-and-their-experiences-on-social-media/.

Centers for Disease Control and Prevention. (2015). *Youth risk behavior survey data.* https://www.cdc.gov/healthyyouth/data/yrbs/index.htm.

Centers for Disease Control and Prevention. (2020). *ADHD throughout the years.* https://www.cdc.gov/ncbddd/adhd/timeline.html.

Chahal, H., Fung, C., Kuhle, S., & Veugelers, P. J. (2013). Availability and night-time use of electronic entertainment and communication devices are associated with short sleep duration and obesity among Canadian children. *Pediatric Obesity, 8*(1), 42–51.

Exelmans, L. & Van den Bulck, J. (2016). Bedtime mobile phone use and sleep in adults. *Social Science and Medicine, 148*, 93–101. https://doi.org/10.1016/j.socscimed.2015.11.037.

Falbe, J., Davison, K. K., Franckle, R. L., Ganter, C., Gortmaker, S. L., Smith, L., & Taveras, E. M. (2015). Sleep duration, restfulness, and screens in the sleep environment. *Pediatrics, 135*(2), 368–75. http://dx.doi.org/10.1542/peds.2014-2306.

Felt, L. & Robb, M. (2016). *Technology addiction: Concern, controversy, and finding balance.* https://www.commonsensemedia.org/sites/default/files/uploads/research/csm_2016_technology_addiction_research_brief_0.pdf.

Gopinath, B., Hardy, L. L., Kifley, A., Baur, L. A., & Mitchell, P. (2014). Activity behaviors in schoolchildren and subsequent 5-yr change in blood pressure. *Medicine and Science in Sports and Exercise, 46*(4), 724–29. http://dx.doi.org/10.1249/MSS.0000000000000166.

Grover, K., Pecor, K., Malkowski, M., & Ming, X. (2016). Effects of instant messaging on school performance in adolescents. *Journal of Child Neurology, 31*(7), 850–57. https://doi.org/10.1177/0883073815624758.

Hettler, B. (1976). *The six dimensions of wellness model.* National Wellness Institute, Inc. http://c.ymcdn.com/sites/www.nationalwellness.org/resource/resmgr/docs/sixdimensionsfactsheet.pdf.

James, C., Weinstein, E., & Mendoza, K. (2019). *Teaching digital citizens in today's world: Research and insights behind the Common Sense K–12 Digital Citizenship Curriculum.* Common Sense Media.

Jiminy. (2019). *Children and sexting—a Jiminy report.* https://blog.jiminy.me/2019/12/17/children-and-sexting-a-jiminy-report/.

Kahne, J., Middaugh, E., & Allen, D. (2015). Youth, new media and the rise of participatory politics. In D. Allen & J. Light (eds.), *From voice to influence: Understanding citizenship in a digital age.* University of Chicago Press.

Kimball, H. & Cohen, Y. (2019). *Children's mental health report: Social media, gaming and mental health.* Child Mind Institute.

Kindt, S., Szász-Janocha, C., Rehbein, F., & Lindenberg, K. (2019). School-related risk factors of internet use disorders. *International Journal of Environmental Research and Public Health, 16*(24), 4938. https://doi.org/10.3390/ijerph16244938.

Lexico Dictionary. (n.d.). Social media. In *Lexico.com dictionary.* https://www.lexico.com/en/definition/social_media.

Macgregor, D. M. (2000). Nintendonitis? A case report of repetitive strain injury in a child as a result of playing computer games. *Scottish Medical Journal, 45,* 5. https://doi.org/10.1177/003693300004500507.

Martin, R., Henderson-Smith, L., Blanco, T., Robinson Graves, M., & Lange, D. (2016). *Making physical health and well-being matter for youth and young adults: Education and prevention.* Substance Abuse and Mental Health Services Administration (SAMHS). https://www.samhsa.gov/sites/default/files/programs_campaigns/wellness_initiative/youth-young-adults-webinar.pdf.

Mattson, K. (2017). *Digital citizenship in action: Empowering students to engage in online communities.* ISTE Publishing.

Meerkerk, G.-J., van den Eijnden, R. J. J. M., Vermulst, A. A., & Garretsen, H. F. L. (2009). The Compulsive Internet Use Scale (CIUS): Some psychometric properties. *CyberPsychology and Behavior, 12*(1), 1–6. https://doi.org/10.1089/cpb.2008.0181.

Mossberger, K., Tolbert, C., & McNeal, R. (2008). *Digital citizenship: The Internet, society, and participation.* MIT Press.

Muresan, R. (2016). *One in 10 visitors of porn sites is under 10 years old.* https://hotforsecurity.bitdefender.com/blog/one-in-10-visitors-of-porn-sites-is-under-10-years-old-16675.html.

Nightingale, C. M., Rudnicka, A. R., Donin, A. S., Sattar, N., Cook, D. G., Whincup, P. H., & Owen, C. G. (2017). Screen time is associated with adiposity and insulin resistance in children. *Archives of Disease in Childhood, 102*(7), 612–16. http://dx.doi.org/10.1136/archdischild2016-312016.

Paruthi, S., Brooks, L. J., D'Ambrosio, C., Hall, W. A., Katagal, S., Lloyd, R. M., Malow, B. A., Maski, K., Nichols, C., Quan, S. F., Rosen, C. L., Troester, M. M., & Wise, M. S. (2016). Consensus statement of the American Academy of Sleep Medicine on the recommended amount of sleep for healthy children: Methodology and discussion. *Journal of Clinical Sleep Medicine, 12,* 1549–61. https://doi.org/10.5664/jcsm.6288.

Ribble, M. & Bailey, G. (2007). *Digital citizenship in schools.* ISTE Publishing.

Rideout, V. (2015). *Common Sense census: Media use by tweens and teens.* Common Sense Media.

Rideout, V. (2017). *The Common Sense census: Media use by kids age zero to eight.* Common Sense Media

Rideout, V. & Fox, S. (2018). *Digital health practices, social media use, and mental well-being among teens and young adults in the U.S.* Hopelab/Well Being Trust.

Rideout, V. & Robb, M. (2018). *Social media, social life: Teens reveal their experiences.* Common Sense Media.

Rideout, V. & Robb, M. B. (2019). *Common Sense census: Media use by tweens and teens.* Common Sense Media.

Schoology. (2020). *The state of digital learning.* https://www.schoology.com/state-of-digital-learning.

Spurr, S., Bally, J., Ogenchuk, M., & Walker, K. (2012). A framework for exploring adolescent wellness. *Pediatric Nursing, 38,* 320–26.

Weiss, M. D., Baer, S., Allan, B. A., Saran, K., & Schibuk, H. (2011). The screens culture: Impact on ADHD. *Attention Deficit and Hyperactive Disorders, 3*, 327–34.

Woods, H. C. & Scott, H. (2016). #Sleepyteens: Social media use in adolescence is associated with poor sleep quality, anxiety, depression and low self-esteem. *Journal of Adolescence, 51*, 41–49. https://doi.org/10.1016/j.adolescence.2016.05.008.

Chapter 6

The Role of Coding

Madison McClung

Jennifer Miller is the new instructional coach for Pine View K–8 School, a large school that is struggling to raise its school grade, especially in reading. For the new school year, Pine View's principal, Greg Jones, set a goal of bringing their reading score up by 10 points. As instructional coach, Jennifer incorporated their new goal into her plans. Along with their reading goals, Pine View has also decided to incorporate coding into their curriculum in an attempt to better align with STEM standards.

Pine View is a low-tech school with two computer labs and to supplement these labs, students are encouraged to bring their own devices to use in class. The teachers often do not incorporate technology in their instruction, and some are apprehensive to use it. When technology is incorporated into the classroom, it is mainly for efficiency of taking tests, interactive games, or doing research. Miller knew if the goal of incorporating coding was going to be successful in the upcoming school year, she would have to get creative. The budget did not allow for a full technology class, so all coding instructions would need to be implemented into the curriculum that was already in place.

Miller and Jones initially were concerned about how their staff would react and if they would be receptive to these new goals. Together they decided to implement reading-based strategies that would lend themselves to providing the foundations of coding. There was a small budget set aside for technology that would be used to purchase licenses to a coding site and other coding tools such as games and robots. These resources would be available to all teachers from kindergarten to eighth grade to be able to incorporate into their curriculum.

As a part of the teachers' back to school professional development, Miller designed a day for the teachers to explore and play with these tools, so they could become familiar with them. Miller presented high-tech, low-tech, and no-tech methods of coding. Teachers were encouraged to participate in the activities and think about them from the perspective of a student.

WHAT IS CODING?

When Miller was originally approached about integrating coding into the curriculum, she was concerned how it would fit in without a traditional technology or STEM class, so she examined the foundations of what coding is all about. Often when teachers and students visualize coding, they think of a complex computer science (CS) task, when in reality, coding is based on simple skills that are taught across the curriculum. Coding in the classroom has been linked to improved problem-solving and analytical reasoning, and students who develop a mastery of coding have an ability and drive to construct, hypothesize, explore, experiment, evaluate, and draw conclusions (Huerta, 2015). By focusing on these standards, it allows coding to be integrated into all grades and subject areas. These skills also align with Bloom's Revised Taxonomy standards, which encourage students to exercise higher-order thinking. The skills are important for school achievement but are also important in daily life, higher education, and careers.

Schools often lack qualified teachers to teach CS; therefore, students often do not have the opportunities to learn these skills. Sixty-three percent of K–12 principals and 74 percent of superintendents, who do not have CS in their school or district, say one reason they do not offer CS is the lack of teachers with the necessary skills to teach it (Google Inc. & Gallup Inc., 2016).

When we examine the skills that coding develops, we see significant integration with other subjects that will lead to a greater demand for CS skills. From coding comes computational thinking that allows the learner to approach a problem from an innovative and strategic point of view. Computational thinking can start with a simple task such as, "The front door to the classroom is locked, what are some other ways we can get in?" Most students may say to unlock the door, but others may suggest getting the keys from the janitor, trying to open a window, or using other tools to open the door. It is crucial that students see that there is more than one way to approach a problem and understand the importance of developing various methods for completing a task. When coding, students could be presented with the simple task of moving an object from point A to point B, but coding requires the students to understand the steps they need to take to accomplish the objective not just the final goal. Some students could program the object to slide from one point to another, while others might choose to have the object flash and appear at the next point; each is a valid answer, but each process requires different steps. It is important to shift the mindset of coding from people who have a specific degree to anyone who has the ability to code. This mindset shift will enable teachers to have the confidence to teach the skills of coding as well as encourage students that they have the ability to code.

HOW TO GET STARTED WITH CODING

Coding in the classroom can also look different depending on what apps, programs, and grades are being considered. Coding can start off very basic with children as young as five years old. Programs such as CodeSpark Academy are used for early elementary coding because the students use pictures to code rather than words or coding language. Students learn the process of coding by making up a scenario then picking the objects to complete the scenario (codeSpark, 2020).

The next step would be coding with blocks. This is the most common form of coding that can be easily used for any grade, typically second grade and up. By coding with blocks, learners use traditional coding statements without the coding formatting. These programs such as Scratch (Scratch, 2020) and Code.org (Code.org, 2020) work by assembling blocks to create a command. The co-founders of Scratch stated, "For us, coding is not a set of technical skills but a new type of literacy and personal expression, valuable for everyone, much like learning to write. We see coding as a new way for people to organize, express, and share their ideas" (Resnick & Seigel, 2015, para. 3). These blocks can be simple or complex, depending on the level of the student. This also would allow for differentiation in the classroom since students would be able to work at their own comfort level.

The last level would be students using full-text codes. This full-text code is traditionally what would be seen in a job or college. The student would be writing code in full formatting and sentences. Apps such as Code Academy (Code Academy, 2020) or *Google Digital Applied Skills* (Google Digital Applied Skills, 2020) give the students opportunities to use a textual format to create a code model.

TEACHING FOR THE
TWENTY-FIRST-CENTURY STUDENT

Miller and Jones knew that in order to fulfill their goals of boosting literacy and integrating coding, they would have to integrate coding across the curriculum. Technology and coding are undoubtedly the key to success for our twenty-first-century students. In jobs, universities, and even the military, computational thinking is an essential skill. By teaching students coding in the K–12 classroom, teachers are able to spark students' interest so that they can follow the path to a career with coding. In the United States alone it is estimated that there will be 1.4 million jobs in the computer field, by the end of 2020 including coding, engineering, and data mining, but the current data indicate there will be only 400,000 college students majoring in CS (Davis, 2013). Not all students will enter a coding or a technology field, but the skills from coding can be acquired and used in any career.

Students are able to use coding for a multitude of different interests. Students can invent apps, create games, design a website, program a robot, or even design an artificial intelligence program. These are often not state-mandated and tested skills, so coding and CS often take a backseat to those areas assessed by mandatory state assessments in many schools. Hadi Partovi, founder of Code.org, stated, "Ten to 15 years from now, computer science will be as important as reading and math, and we'll be wondering why we didn't change sooner" (Davis, 2013, para. 18). Education needs to be evolving as quickly as the world outside of the educational setting so that our students are prepared and adaptable. These coding languages are already becoming second nature to students and they are finding ways to participate in these activities in clubs, extracurriculars, or even at home. As educators recognize their students' successes with coding, they can sharpen learners' skills to help them develop proficiency.

The International Society for Technology Education, also known as ISTE, recognizes seven standards for educating our twenty-first-century students. The ISTE student standards are Empowered Learner, Digital Citizen, Knowledge Constructor, Innovative Designer, Computational Thinker, Creative Communicator, and Global Collaborator (ISTE, 2016). The standard of Computational Thinker is where ISTE encompasses many of the principles involved in coding. The role of developing computational thinking allows learners to abstractly look at a situation and develop innovative solutions. Computational thinking is often implemented as a goal to be developed later in technology courses after a student has achieved the prior ISTE standards.

Some of the activities that are included in the standard of computational thinking are understanding automation of apps, developing algorithms, and debugging coding. These activities allow the students to think beyond the surface application and think more deeply about the why something is occurring. For example, when a student is debugging code, they will have a bug, or an error, in their lines of code, so they will have to determine what went wrong. This error can be as simple as forgetting to put a period somewhere to using the wrong statement construction. The skill of "debugging" can be used in the classroom to have students examine an event that did not have the expected outcome, and students can pinpoint the change and predict what would happen if a different event occurred.

CURRICULUM INTEGRATION

Computational thinking is not just or all about CS. The educational benefits of being able to think computationally—starting with the use of abstractions—enhance and reinforce intellectual skills, and thus can be transferred to any domain (Wing, 2014). Wing explores the basis of coding and its natural integration across the curriculum. So where would one start the task of coding in the classroom?

Wing encourages students to begin by following simple directions and building a strong reading foundation. This task encourages students to break down an event and analyze the cause and effect. Since cause and effect or conditional statements are the basis for coding, students will need to become familiar with the process so that they can translate these into coding a program. Coding is the new literacy for the twenty-first century (Bers et al., 2019). Statements or commands of coding are based on the following type of directions such as "if x equals 2 then y will turn yellow" or "when x is clicked y will rotate 15° clockwise." These statements are based upon simple cause and effect relationships. Students see an event happening and then must determine the reaction. Students will be able to determine that when the object is "x" and the action is "clicking y" and then the object is described at the "15° clockwise" position. Developing the understanding of these coding commands can help to expand students' understanding of English syntax by having students determine verbs, adjectives, and nouns in the texts they are reading.

Miller wanted to help teachers develop a goal for each subject that would lend itself to the integration of coding and computational thinking. Each teacher had to examine their curriculum and determine a subject that the learners would have significant content knowledge about. As students became comfortable with the content, teachers were encouraged to take them to the next level by integrating coding skills into their lessons.

One example of a lesson could be integrating coding would be a math lesson. If students are learning about conditional statements, then they can use a coding software such as code.org or Scratch and create a code using conditional statements. Students could create a game where every time a player clicked a blue dot, for example, they would receive a point, and every time they clicked a yellow dot, they would lose a point. The code would read, "If blue dot is clicked, then add 1 point," and "If a yellow dot is clicked then subtract 1 point."

Another example of a lesson involving coding skills would be a teacher reading a story to the class and then taking each main event and posting it around the room. Learners then would have to draw a map using directionals for their partners to follow to put the events in the correct order. This might look something like this, "Start at event A, take 5 steps left and one step forward to reach event B." This activity requires students to use their sequential thinking and directional skills to organize the events from the story. Students need to identify the task, how each event is related to each other, how one event leads to the next, and how to clearly communicate that to their partners. Coding is not an activity that is only computer-based because the thinking can be integrated into any subject area.

As coding and CS are integrated across the curriculum, students will become more comfortable with the ideas and expectations involved. Computational thinking is an approach to solving problems that is expressed in a way that can be implemented by a computer. Through practicing these skills, students can become not merely tool users but also tool builders (Barr & Stephenson, 2011).

NONCOMPUTER CODING ALTERNATIVES AND CODING MOVEMENTS

Robots and other coding devices are becoming increasingly popular in schools. Robots and other coding objects were once seen as only an extracurricular, but they are rapidly finding their way into the everyday classroom curriculum. Robots can take on a number of different roles in the learning process, with varying levels of involvement in the content learning task. The choice depends on the content, the instructor, the type of student, and the nature of the learning activity (Mubin et al., 2013). The most common use of technology evidenced previously in education is the use of assistive technologies such as assistive keyboard or speech dictators. However, the classroom "robot" has evolved to encompass all aspects of the classroom, seeping into all subjects.

The small but mighty Ozobot is a common device that can be used across all grades and subjects. The Ozobot is a small interactive toy that uses its sensors to recognize commands presented through different colored combination lines (Fojtik, 2017). By interacting with this basic robot, students are able to develop a sequence that the Ozobot will follow. All that students need are markers, a piece of white paper, and the Ozobot, and they can program it to complete a series of activities from the list of possible sequences. The use and logic is simple for any grade and could be used in any subject. An example of a possible coding project would be a class using the Ozobot to sequence the events in the Civil War. Students draw a color sequenced line from written explanations of the events or pictures of the events and the Ozobot travels to each one in the correct order.

Cubetto is another classroom tool that offers an alternative to computer-based coding. Cubetto is planned for learners three to nine years of age. Students place command tiles on a board and when the "Cubetto" passes over the boxes on the floor map corresponding to the code, it responds to the commands. This program offers simple commands that work together to make a program sequence. The Cubetto program is based on stories that students help Cubetto to solve. These stories help to engage student readers and encourage them to practice computational thinking (Primo, 2020). Children will attempt to make the Cubetto's actions correspond with the story. For example, if the Cubetto has to swim across the ocean, the students would construct a sequence that simulates swimming across the correct location. This not only will help with reading comprehension but also allows the students to learn about constructing directionals, developing sequencing, understanding the compass rose, and following instructions.

Bloxels are a low-tech tangible way to code in the classroom. Bloxels is paired with a tablet and learners tangibly code with blocks to program the digital games. Tangible learning invites users to experience and understand thinking processes such as design thinking and computational thinking through rapid prototyping with tangible media (Lee, 2016). With Bloxels, the coding is determined fully based upon the placement of colored blocks in a grid. The colored blocks represent a specific function and act together to form a coding sequence. In the Bloxles program, students can, for example, pick up a green block to indicate land and a blue block to indicate water. This tangible learning is something that most coding programs cannot offer because of the more digital aspects. When the blocks are scanned via camera through the tablet app, the sequence is translated into a playable game. This hands-on learning appeals to students who want to physically build the code. This can be used among all ages and abilities of learners and can be a great starting point for learning to code.

Osmo is another tool that allows for a variety of coding experience for elementary aged learners. By using a tablet and the Osmo kits, children as young as three can program in a multitude of different ways. Osmo is a "reflective artificial intelligence" technology where a student creates something on a mat and it is reflected in the Osmo app (Osmo, 2020). Students can see their creations come to life and interact with them on their tablet. One feature that Osmo offers is a "Words" app. The "Words" app shows a sequence of letters that make a word, and students must manipulate the materials to create the missing letter on the Osmo mat. It is then reflected back to the tablet, and the information is displayed on the table using the app. Osmo uses a technique called reflective artificial intelligence technology (RAIT) that merges play-based and technological interventions into a single tablet app (Broda & Frank, 2015). The RAIT technique gives a deeper purpose to the "play" and is developed to connect to deepening education skills.

CONCLUSION

The idea of teaching coding can at times seem to be overwhelming, but there are many coding options to help ease teachers and students into the coding process. Hour of Code (Hour of Code, 2020) is an international movement that is aimed at teaching the fundamentals of coding for one hour. Hour of Code is hosted by Code.org and breaks down coding so that anyone can learn how to code. There is an hour-long course that can be implemented at any time of the year and is geared toward people who have never coded before. This introduction familiarizes students with coding and its skills of computational thinking, innovative problem-solving, and enhancing logic and creativity. Code.org also hosts a Computer Science Week that typically falls in the second week of December. This week is geared toward introducing coding to students and raising the awareness of the benefits of coding. Schools across the globe are encouraged to participate (Computer Science Education Week, 2020).

Girls Who Code is aimed at closing the school gender gap in coding and has served over 300,000 girls across the world. In 1995, 37 percent of computer scientists were women. Today, this percentage has dropped to 24 percent. This percentage will continue to decline if we do nothing. We know that the biggest drop off of girls in CS is between the ages of thirteen and seventeen (Girls Who

Code, 2020). In an attempt to address this issue, many schools have implemented Girls Who Code as a club and many use the varied resources provided by the organization.

REFLECT AND APPLY ACTIVITIES

6.1. Develop a "no tech" coding assignment for a class and grade level of your choice where technology has not been traditionally used. Look back at ISTE's standards for computational thinkers and how that can be integrated into your curriculum.
6.2. As an educator, choose one of the mentioned coding programs that you have not already used and create an account to practice coding yourself. Choose a project that you can complete alongside your students. This will encourage conversations and troubleshooting with your students and allow you to experience what the students are experiencing.

REFERENCES

Girls Who Code. (2020). The gender gap in computer is getting worse. https://girlswhocode.com/about-us/.
Barr, V. & Stephenson, C. (2011, March). Bringing computational thinking to K–12: What is involved and what is the role of the computer science education community? *ACM Inroads*, *2*(1), 48–55. https://id.iste.org/docs/nets-refresh-toolkit/bringing-ct-to-k-12.pdf.
Bers, M. U., González-González, C. & Belén Armas-Torres, M. (2019, September). Coding as a playground: Promoting positive learning experiences in childhood classrooms. *Computers& Education*, *138*, 130–45. doi: https://doi.org/10.1016/j.compedu.2019.04.013.
Broda, M. & Frank, A. (2015). Learning beyond the screen: Assessing the impact of reflective artificial intelligence technology on the development of emergent literacy skills. In *Proceedings of E-Learn: World Conference on E-Learning in Corporate, Government, Healthcare, and Higher Education* (pp. 753–58). Association for the Advancement of Computing in Education (AACE).
Code Academy. (2020). Learn to code—for free. https://www.codecademy.com/.
Code.org. (2020). Learn computer science, change the world. https://code.org/.

codeSpark. (2020). codeSpark Academy. https://accounts.codespark. com/ ?utm_campaign=9658925487&utm_source=google_ads&utm_medium= cpc&utm_term=g&utm_content=codespark%20academy&gclid=CjwKCA jwmMX4BRAAEiwA-zM4JsLr9np9JZ_4XWeDPD6wXV4IJZTqm_ yqgWqFIhJQDnwXgS-j-ySl6RoCBnkQAvD_BwE&utm_expid=.5PK UKsPqRDiokHHMEnbIqg.0&utm_referrer=https%3A%2F%2Fwww. google.com%2F.

Computer Science Education Week. (2020). Hour of code events around the world. https://csedweek.org/.

Davis, M. (2013, June). Computer coding lessons expanding for K–12 students. *Education Week, 6*(3), 30–31. http://worldwideworkshop.org/pdfs/ Globaloria_Press_EducationWeek_ComputerCodingLessonsforKids.pdf.

Fojtik, R. (2017, November). The Ozobot and education of programming. *New Trends and Issues Proceedings on Humanities and Social Sciences, 4*(5), 8–16. https://www.researchgate.net/publication/321424090_The_ Ozobot_and_education_of_programming.

Google Digital Applied Skills. (2020). Teaching resources for digital skills. https://applieddigitalskills.withgoogle.com/en/teaching-resources-2? pvar=xyz&src=cpc-google-20180531-applied.digital.skills-hsms-ins- &gclid=EAIaIQobChMIkJaB9u3X6gIVk4zlCh39cQKdEAAYASAAEg KGvvD_BwE#.

Google Inc. & Gallup Inc. (2016). Trends in the state of computer science in U.S. K–12 schools. http://goo.gl/j291E0.

Hour of Code. (2020). Join the largest learning event in history. https:// hourofcode.com/us.

Huerta, M. (2015, April). Coding in the classroom: A long-overdue inclusion. *Edutopia.* https://www.edutopia.org/blog/coding-classroom- long-overdue-inclusion-merle-huerta.

International Society for Technology in Education. (2016). ISTE standards for students. https://www.iste.org/standards/for-students.

Lee, K. T. (2016). Use of tangible learning in stem education. *Association for Computing Machinery.* https://doi.org/10.1145/2999508.3008582.

Mubin, O., Stevens, C. J., Shahid, S., Mahmud, A. A., & Dong, J. J. (2013). A review of the applicability of robots in education. *Technology for Education and Learning, 1,* 1–7. http://roila.org/wp-content/uploads/ 2013/07/209-0015.pdf.

Osmo. (2020). Transforming how children learn. https://www.iste.org/ standards/for-students.

Primo. (2020). Cubetto. https://www.primotoys.com/cubetto/.

Resnick, M. & Siegal, D. (2015, January). A different approach to coding: How kids are making and remaking themselves from Scratch. *International*

Journal of People-Oriented Programming. Bright. https://bright
themag.com/a-different-approach-to-coding-d679b06d83a.

Scratch. (2020). Scratch—imagine, program, share. https://scratch.mit.edu/.

Wing, J. M. (2014, January). Computational thinking benefits society. http://
www.computacional.com.br/files/Wing/WING 2014—Computational
Thinking Benefits Society.pdf.

Chapter 7

Breaking Down Barriers to Achievement through Universal Design for Learning and Assistive Technology

Lori Goehrig, Maureen Kasa, and Jessie Brown

Minnie is the assistant principal in charge of curriculum at Oak Ridge Elementary School. The group of students with disabilities did not demonstrate significant growth last year, so she wanted to make sure that did not happen again. She wondered how to best support the general education teachers in the new school year. She knew that technology would be a priority for her. In the past school year, the use of computers, laptops, and iPads was somewhat limited in the classrooms, but this fall Minnie's school was implementing 1:1 technology.

In preparation for teacher training, Minnie decides to learn more about the technology available in the district. She knows firsthand how important technology can be for students. Minnie's younger cousin had been enrolled in general education classrooms and was assigned a 1:1 assistant. In addition to helping him navigate physical barriers, the assistant provided support by reading assignments and textbooks, acted as a scribe for written assignments, and submitted work electronically to his teachers. During his senior year, Minnie's cousin decided that he would like to go to community college. The IEP team realized he was not prepared to transition to college. Not only did he not use any instructional technology, but the team had also neglected to consider assistive technology that would have enabled him to become a more independent student. To help teachers implement 1:1 technology for all students, Minnie will need to become familiar with the technology and applications provided by the district and assistive technology options for students with disabilities.

INSTRUCTIONAL TECHNOLOGY AND UNIVERSAL DESIGN FOR LEARNING

Minnie decided that training the teachers to use a Universal Design for Learning (UDL) approach to lesson planning would provide a good starting point. Allison Posey (2019) described the impact of using UDL to support all learners. She stated that UDL "can help you make sure that the greatest range of students can access and engage in learning—not just certain students" (para. 7). She further explained that a strength of UDL was that specific tools or technologies were not needed to follow UDL's principles. Instead, students were able to choose from the tools and resources that were already available.

To learn about what technology resources are available in the district, Minnie reached out to the building technology specialist and district instructional technology department. She wanted to make sure she knew what the district policy was and whether there were any specific tools teachers were encouraged or even mandated to use in their classroom. While Minnie was preparing information about UDL, she met with her building technology specialist. She knew she had Word and PowerPoint on her school computer, but she was not sure of what other features were built into Office 365. The building technology specialist explained that Word, PowerPoint, and Excel have embedded assistive technology tools such as speech-to-text and text-to-speech within their software programs. These Microsoft Learning Tools would be a wonderful way for teachers to support students with varying learning disabilities within the general education classroom.

Minnie was amazed to discover the accessibility features that had been built into the Windows operating system. These would be wonderful ways for teachers to support their learners. Tools embedded in this operating system include word prediction, which would be particularly helpful for both students who struggle with spelling and those needing reduced keystrokes because of physical challenges. Additionally, students with sensory disorders could be supported through ease of access for vision, hearing, and interaction. For those individuals facing vision challenges, the screen could be enlarged, made brighter, or even read to the student. Closed captioning, mono sound, and live call transcription are features that may be beneficial for those individuals with hearing challenges. Those individuals with dyslexia, seizures, autism, and other cognitive differences will benefit from such innovative tools as dictation (Microsoft, 2020). Similar accessibility features are also included in the Apple operating system (Access Computing, 2020). As technology continues to develop, Microsoft and Apple are updating accessibility features for vision, physical and motor issues, and hearing deficits to support individuals with sensory disorders. Their websites can provide information related to recent updates.

ASSISTIVE TECHNOLOGY FOR STUDENTS WITH DISABILITIES

In addition to learning about the instructional technology that was available, Minnie wanted to learn more about the other options available with assistive technology. She spoke with Jane, one of the special education teachers in her building, and Jane shared with Minnie the Florida Department of Education's Technical Assistance Paper (TAP): Assistive Technology for Students with Disabilities (2013). This document was developed based on the Individuals with Disabilities Education Act of 2004 and was created to provide guidance to Florida school districts regarding assistive technology. Assistive technology includes "any item, piece of equipment or product system—whether acquired commercially off the shelf, modified or customized—used to increase, maintain or improve the functional capabilities of a student with a disability" (p. 1). Since assistive technology is continually evolving, the TAP does not contain a list of the specific assistive devices.

Minnie knew that annually, Individualized Education Plan (IEP) teams met to consider the services and technology devices that would be appropriate for supporting a student's educational plan. During this meeting the team discussed the student's abilities, needs, and any technology already being used. The team used this information to guide their decisions. The IEP team at her school had a list of four questions to assist the members in deciding on appropriate assistive technology.

- What should the student to be able to do in the areas of writing, reading, communicating, seeing, and hearing that the student is not currently able to do because of the disability?
- How effectively is the student currently able to complete tasks using particular strategies or accommodations?
- Is there assistive technology (e.g., devices, tools, hardware, or software) that is currently being used to support the student with these tasks?
- Would assistive technology help the student perform this skill more easily, efficiently, in a less restrictive environment, or perform it more independently (Center for Parent Information and Resources, 2017)?

Decisions about assistive technology should start with the student and then include members of the IEP team, since they are the individuals directly working with the student. Additional support can be provided as recommended by the IEP team (Florida Department of Education, 2013). The SETT Framework is a tool that Minnie's school uses to help teams identify effective assistive technology. SETT stands for Student, Environments, Tasks, and Tools. The framework is based on the idea that to develop an appropriate system of Tools, teams must first develop an understanding of the student, the usual environments where the student learns, and the tasks the student should be able to do or learn to do to actively participate in the teaching and learning processes. When the needs, abilities, and interests of the Student, the details of the Environments, and the specific Tasks required are fully explored, teams are prepared to consider the needs to be addressed by the system of tools. These tools can include supports such as services, strategies, and accommodations or modifications (Zabala, 2005).

As Minnie prepared to share these ideas with the faculty, she wondered how to explain the differences between UDL and the term "assistive technology." She decided to include an example of a student with a reading disability who struggled with decoding and comprehending written texts. An assistive technology lens might view this difficulty as an individual problem where the student's reading disability is interfering with his ability to master content and demonstrate knowledge (Rose et al., 2005). One possible solution might be to include e-books found on Bookshare.org, which have accessibility features built into the reading materials, thus providing the student with disabilities more independence.

A UDL lens would view this as an issue rooted in the school or classroom environment. For example, the overreliance on printed text can often lead to a lack of engagement and content mastery for students. In this view, the limitations reside with the curriculum and not the student (Rose et al., 2005). A UDL solution could include providing all students with an array of options for viewing and manipulating print and nonprint forms of text. Students might enlarge or color text for viewing, have text read aloud, or use closed captioning. The options are endless and available to all.

Although UDL and assistive technology have unique perspectives, they are not incongruous. Together, the two views provide educators with support in how to design accessible learning environments that are useful for all students (Rose et al., 2005).

INSTRUCTIONAL AND ASSISTIVE TECHNOLOGY SOLUTIONS FOR STUDENTS WITH LEARNING DISABILITIES

Teachers often embrace the idea of reducing barriers for all students using the UDL approach. They feel students will be more likely to utilize needed technology if other students are using it too. Knowing that some students will use technology by choice while others will need the technology to be successful in their educational environment, leaders, like Minnie, must ensure they provide their teachers with professional development opportunities to learn how to support all students using technology.

During the summer, the teachers are designing their learning environments to support and encourage engaged learners. A concern the teachers have voiced is if the one-to-one technology will be available to students and whether the changes they are planning will be enough to reduce barriers for all students. In preparation for training, Minnie made sure her general education teachers read IEPs for incoming students. She asked them to note which students had assistive technology documented on their IEPs and to list the assistive technology for each student. During the new school year, Minnie will encourage teachers to implement assistive and instructional technology combined with UDL. Minnie feels confident that the teachers will be ready for students needing text-to-speech as the preplanning session will include how to use the Office 365's text-to-speech software. She knows students with learning disabilities can benefit from this instructional technology available to all students and that this same technology may be considered assistive technology if the IEP team determines the student needs that technology to receive a Free and Appropriate Public Education (FAPE).

In addition to students with learning disabilities using readily available tools, such as Microsoft Learning Tools, Minnie noted that the students with significant cognitive challenges required assistive technology beyond those tools readily available to all learners. These students were in the process of learning to become less dependent on adults and more independent using the tools provided. Minnie knew that the teachers would need to work closely with the special education department to determine accessibility for these students with differing learning, physical, vision, and hearing needs. With more technology in the hands of students, the need for training, and the understanding of how to use the technology, is extremely critical for both students' and teachers' success. Minnie would make understanding how technology can help students with disabilities, especially those with significant challenges, a priority when planning for the new academic year.

ASSISTIVE TECHNOLOGY SOLUTIONS FOR STUDENTS WITH COMMUNICATION DISORDERS

Minnie knows there are incoming students with significant challenges, so she is concerned about meeting their needs on day one of the new school year. Some of these students have difficulty communicating as proficiently as their same-age peers and she wonders how best to prepare the teachers to help these students learn words and interact with peers and adults in the classroom. Teachers will be concerned about how these students will participate in class discussions, get along with their peers, or complete assignments.

In attempting to meet this need, Minnie decides to contact the school's speech-language pathologist, or SLP, an expert in communication-related disorders, to have her provide a session for the teachers. During the session, the SLP would explain that communication takes many forms and can include gestures, objects, vocalizations, words, signs, pictures, or symbols. These symbols could be spoken or written words as well as those in picture form. For each student using an alternate form of communication, all individuals who interact with the student must be using the same shared system. In this way, the student learns that this is his form of communication. When others "talk" to a student using his system, he not only realizes this is his voice but also learns the vocabulary and navigation of the system (ASHA, n.d.).

The SLP also plans to explain the technology that is available for those students struggling with the ability to express their thoughts and ideas. Augmentative and alternative communication (AAC) is the term used to describe numerous ways to express words and ideas for those individuals unable to produce speech. AAC may enhance the limited speech the student already possesses, or it may compensate for the inability to produce intelligible speech (ASHA, n.d.). AAC can take a variety of forms, including paper-based communication boards with symbols, tangible objects, 3D printed symbols, or high-tech communication systems with robust communication software.

Many AAC users can directly select the messages on their communication systems by pointing to symbols on a communication board or tapping buttons or cells on a high-tech communication device. Other AAC users with motor and physical limitations, like a couple of the students in Minnie's school, are unable to use direct select to access their devices, but they are able to control the pointer or cursor with eye movements (eye gaze) or head movements (head tracking with a reflective dot placed on the head, eyeglasses, etc.). One student needs the communication device to scan through, then highlight options before activating a switch to select the desired message (switch scanning). Another student who is unable to access his device using these methods expresses his thoughts and ideas using partner-assisted scanning. This strategy pairs the student with a communication partner. The partner reads through the list of possible choices, stopping when the AAC user indicates, "Yes, that's it." The SLP will be a great ally for those students with a severe communication disorder by helping assess the need for assistive technology and providing further direction and assistance when trialing different AAC systems with the student.

When a student already has a high-tech communication system in place, the SLP can provide training to all staff working with this student in the use of the communication system. She can also reach out to the district's Assistive Technology Department or the vendor for assistance.

This training may include an explanation and demonstration of the layout of the language system on the device, how to operate the device, such as turning it off and on, adjusting the volume, and editing or adding information, and the student's access method, so all staff members have a working knowledge of the assistive technology being used.

The SLP will also provide information about the student's skill level with the system, the support needed for successful implementation, and strategies to promote the student's communicative independence. Gallagher and Litton (2014) offer educators guidance on how to ensure the success of AAC systems in the classroom, including:

- Make the device accessible, place it in front of the student, and have it ready to be used.
- Make sure your perceptions and expectations are high. Presume the student is capable.
- Plan ahead to make implementation successful by knowing the layout of the device, what words are available, and where they can be found. Teach your students to ask and answer questions, make comments, express opinions, greet others, and socialize using the vocabulary available on the device.
- Frame your questions, comments, or interactions, so the student can answer using the available words.
- Expect the student to use the communication device. Tell him to use his device because you don't understand what he's trying to tell you.
- Model use of the device. Use the device when you are talking to show the student how he could say it; this helps the student learn

language and the language system of the device. Students using AAC need the same modeling of language as is typical for young children learning to talk. If we expect our students to communicate via symbols, we need to communicate with them using these symbols.

ASSISTIVE TECHNOLOGY SOLUTIONS FOR STUDENTS WITH SENSORY DISORDERS

Minnie realizes this year her school will be serving some students with sensory and motor disabilities. She knows some of the teachers have never taught a student who is deaf or hard-of-hearing (DHH), has a visual impairment (VI), or those receiving occupational (OT) or physical therapy (PT) as a related service.

As Minnie thinks about the challenges these teachers will face, she decides to reach out to the specialists in each area to make sure the teachers will be prepared. They need to know how the disabilities might affect a student and how they could support these students in their classrooms. After talking with both the itinerant teacher of the deaf and hard-of-hearing and the itinerant teacher of the visually impaired assigned to her school, Minnie realizes that students with sensory impairments might miss out on classroom discussions and casual conversations because they have difficulty learning incidentally and must be directly taught those skills their typical peers learn by listening to others in their environment and observing their surroundings.

The school's occupational and physical therapists provide more information about the challenges students with motor issues face. This is an important area because Minnie knows that movement is essential to learning. Children learn by experiencing their world through each of their senses. They need opportunities to move around, try new things, and learn through trial and error (Dotson-Renta, 2016). Each of the specialists stresses that students with sensory or motor impairments are unique, and each student requires strategies or tools designed specifically for their individual needs. This information will help the teachers feel more confident knowing who to contact for support when a student with these unique needs enters their classroom.

ASSISTIVE TECHNOLOGY SOLUTIONS FOR STUDENTS WITH SIGNIFICANT COGNITIVE DISABILITIES

Minnie knows that students with significant cognitive disabilities create challenges for general education and special education teachers in the areas of reading and writing. However, research in emergent literacy shows that students with significant disabilities, including those with complex communication needs, benefit from many of the same literacy activities as typically developing children (Erickson, 2020).

The special education teachers at Minnie's school use many of the same types of literacy activities used with typically developing children; however, they also use alternative strategies and low-tech tools, such as communication boards, to teach reading and facilitate language and communication acquisition. These alternative shared reading strategies, designed for the student's specific needs, enable these learners to actively engage in literacy activities. The special education teachers also recommend that during independent reading students should access the curricular concepts and information through text geared more toward their reading abilities. The occupational therapist and physical therapist recommended e-books via Tarheel Reader, an online library of beginning reading texts. Using this site, students can access books using a mouse, touch screen, alternative pointing devices, AAC devices, or with switches (Tar Heel Reader, n.d.).

Alternative strategies are also available to teach emergent writers. Predictable chart writing supports interaction and teaches communication during a common academic routine, helping all students be successful in the writing process. It can easily be differentiated to support individual learning needs. It is modeled writing, which is especially important for students learning the concept of putting thoughts to paper. Independent writing for students who are unable to hold a pencil or use a keyboard on a computer or an iPad may use alternate access methods, such as eye gaze, head tracking, or switch scanning. For learners unable to effectively use these access methods independently, partner-assisted scanning could be utilized. For this strategy, the students only need to have a way to express, "yes, that's the one," as their communication partner scans through the choices.

Assistive technology strategies and tools are available to increase, maintain, and improve functioning for students with disabilities. Adaptive switches are a significant asset for students with the most complex physical needs. Switches figuratively, and literally, can open doors for learners. They can make a complex movement simple. A mouse click, swipe, or tap may seem like simple flicks of the index finger, but for some students with fine motor deficits, this is nearly impossible. A switch connected to a computer, an iPad, or a communication device makes the connection possible and provides students with the ability to work more independently at home or school (Enabling Devices, n.d.).

Students face barriers like these every day in the classroom. Teachers need to understand that just because a student is unable to hold a traditional pencil, that does not mean he cannot write. It is important to identify the barriers and figure out ways around them. Using technology to think outside the box can break down these once immovable barriers.

Minnie understands that it is vital for teachers to consider all aspects of a student's school experience because access is not just limited to academics. Every time students navigate the halls, play at recess, eat lunch, or socialize with their friends, they may need adaptations or modifications. Educators must always be looking for ways to create more with less. It is the nature of the job. So, it is not a stretch to say thinking outside the box is a way of life for most teachers. Educators who have students with more complex needs know all too well the challenge in equipping students with the tools they need to set them up for success. Meeting this challenge and providing students with these tools not only supports success in the classroom, but it also provides all students with a voice in their education (Castelo, 2020).

Minnie decided that it would be helpful to include in the session a few specific examples of ways to increase independence to make the challenges these students face more evident. The first example would be Jeff, a student with mobility issues. He needs more assistance to make academic progress, but he can access e-books independently using a switch. He can also use a switch to access other classroom tasks on the computer. Interactive lessons that are switch accessible, such as Monarch Teaching Technologies' Vizzle (Vizzle, 2020) or

Inclusive Technologies' *HelpKidzLearn* (HelpKidsLearn, 2017), will be critical for helping Jeff make academic gains. In addition to these high-tech solutions, many low-tech solutions exist to help Jeff develop independence in daily classroom activities. Jeff's teacher wants him to be able to participate fully when using classroom tools. She thinks it will help Jeff to use a highlighter to indicate his answers; however, he is unable to hold the highlighter independently because he needs a larger surface to grasp. The occupational therapist uses items within the environment to create customized AT solutions. Given Jeff's physical limitations, she develops a low-tech solution by poking two holes in a tennis ball and placing the highlighter through the holes. The solution provides Jeff with a larger area to grip, thus allowing him to complete his assignment independently.

Another student, Lisa, is facing challenges building and maintaining relationships with her peers. Her teacher is especially worried about Lisa being able to participate in classroom leisure activities as part of the positive behavior management system. Lisa needs to learn how to make choices and interact with friends. The school social worker suggests using games to facilitate peer socialization, but Lisa has limited physical mobility and speech. The technology specialist recommends that since Lisa uses a switch, she could use the Microsoft's Xbox adaptive controller to connect a switch to enable her to play video games with her peers. The adaptive controller has multiple ports, so Lisa's friends can play along with her allowing her to interact more easily with her peers.

ASSISTIVE TECHNOLOGY SOLUTIONS: COMMUNITY PARTNERS

The Maker Movement is giving out-of-the-box thinkers a whole new dimension to explore. The movement values human passion, capability, and the ability to make things happen and solve problems anywhere, anytime (Martinez, 2019). The basis behind the movement is that Assistive Technology (AT) users can collaborate with engineers and technologists to help them with everyday tasks. High school science, technology, engineering, and mathematics (STEM) and robotics students have the skills necessary to create innovative solutions for the AT users (ATMakers, n.d.).

The goal for every teacher is to promote student independence, but that independence may look different for every student. In thinking about students' use of classroom tools, Minnie knows teachers may need alternative solutions. She reaches out to her son's high school robotics team to challenge them to come up with AT solutions. She contacts the coach and sets up a time for the team to meet the students. They discuss the unique barriers these learners face. The robotics team is excited about the challenge. They design different prototypes and use 3D printers to print them. The team then encourages the students to try out their solutions. They identify additional barriers and possible improvements to their prototypes. This process happens multiple times before the students can enjoy the solutions developed specifically to address their challenges. Not only does the partnership help their student, but it also makes a community connection that may not have happened otherwise. The high school students can positively impact a student's life by coming up with a solution to a real-world problem.

Just as Microsoft is changing the perspective of game designers by embracing Joe Gerstandt's statement, "If you do not intentionally, deliberately and proactively include, you will unintentionally exclude" (University of Nebraska–Lincoln, n.d., para. 1), educators are changing their approach to classroom design. Teachers are now looking at classrooms in a whole new way. They are noticing barriers their students could face and are now adopting a UDL strategy when designing their classrooms.

CONCLUSION

When educators use the UDL framework for classroom planning, students can choose from the available tools and resources. When those technologies do not reduce the barriers to learning for students with disabilities, assistive technology options must be considered. The assistive technology consideration process is a critical component of the IEP team's annual review. Teams must discuss the student's progress within the current education program and consider what alternative strategies or tools might enable the student to perform tasks more efficiently and with less dependence on others. Once assistive technology is in place, teams must develop an implementation plan to manage and maintain the technology's use across school environments to ensure long-term success of the tools. Also, IEP teams must remain aware that instructional and assistive technologies are continually evolving, and new solutions become available. Team members must continue to ask questions to find solutions for their students. The main goal is to help students achieve independence to the best of their ability.

REFLECT AND APPLY ACTIVITIES

7.1. The UDL framework addresses barriers that limit students' learning in a one-size-fits-all curriculum. Companies such as Microsoft, Apple, and Google have embedded accessibility tools into their products to not only support students with disabilities but also give access to all students. Talk with your technology specialist, assistive technology specialist, special education department, or visit websites to determine what accessibility features are embedded in your technology platforms (Microsoft/Apple/Google, etc.). Create a presentation or video to teach others about these accessibility features and tools. Include options for speech-to-text, word prediction, text-to-speech, customizing the display, alternatives for auditory and visual information, and methods for response and navigation.

7.2. Examine the AT consideration process for a student with disabilities that should occur annually during the student's IEP meeting. Identify a student with a significant disability that you feel has needs that are not being met. Collaborate with the student's IEP team and use data-based evidence of the student's academic progress to guide your discussion. Answer the four questions below as your team considers the need for assistive technology for this student.

• What is it we want the student to be able to do within the writing, reading, seeing, communicating, and hearing education program that the student is not able to do because of the disability? Describe the barriers.

• What strategies and accommodations is the student currently using to complete tasks?

- Is there assistive technology (e.g., devices, tools, hardware, or software) currently being used to address this task? What is the assistive technology? How is it being used in the classroom? What supports are needed?
- Would assistive technology help the student perform this skill more easily or efficiently, perform it in the least restrictive environment, or perform it successfully with less personal assistance? How does the AT enable the student to maintain or improve the student's functioning and independence?

REFERENCES

Access Computing. (2020). What accessibility features are available within the Macintosh operating system? https://www.washington.edu/access computing/what-accessibility-features-are-available-within-macintosh-operating-system.

American Speech-Language-Hearing Association (ASHA). (n.d.). *Augmentative and alternative communication (AAC)*. https://www.asha.org/NJC/AAC/#:~:text=Bottom%20Line%3A,disabilities%20and%20their%20communication%20partners.

ATMakers. (n.d.). *Helping makers help others*. https://atmakers.org.

Castelo, M. (2020, March 31). *Using assistive technology to empower students with disabilities*. EdTech Focus on K–12. https://edtechmagazine.com/k12/article/2020/03/using-assistive-technology-empower-students-disabilities-perfcon.

Center for Parent Information and Resources. (2017, November). Considering assistive technology. https://www.parentcenterhub.org/considering-at/.

Dotson-Renta, L. N. (2016, May 19). Why do schools stifle kids' movement? *The Atlantic*. https://www.theatlantic.com/education/archive/2016/05/why-young-kids-learn-through-movement/483408/.

Enabling Devices. (n.d.). Disability adapted switches for people with disabilities. https://enablingdevices.com/product-category/switches/.

Erickson, K. (2020, June). Literacy instruction for students with significant disabilities. *Literacy for all*. https://literacyforallinstruction.ca/presumed-competence/.

Florida Department of Education. (2013). *Technical assistance paper: Assistive technology for students with disabilities* (2013–65). https://info.fldoe.org/docushare/dsweb/Get/Document-6801/dps-2013-65.pdf.

Gallagher, L. & Litton, A. (2014). 54 tips and tricks for implementing alternative and augmentative communication in the classroom. Independent

Living Centre WA. https://ilc.com.au/wp-content/uploads/2014/12/Top-tips-for-implementing-AAC.pdf.

HelpKidsLearn. (2017). Online learning for special education. https://www.helpkidzlearn.com/#.

Martinez, S. (2019, February 11). The maker movement: A learning revolution. *International Society for Technology in Educationi.* https://www.iste.org/explore/In-the-classroom/The-maker-movement%3A-A-learning-revolution.

Microsoft. (2020). Microsoft is committed to accessibility. https://www.microsoft.com/en-us/accessibility.

Posey, A. (2019, August 5). Universal design for learning (UDL): A teacher's guide. *Understood.* https://www.understood.org/en/school-learning/for-educators/universal-design-for-learning/understanding-universal-design-for-learning.

Rose, D. H., Hasselbring, T. S., Stahl, S., & Zabala, J. (2005). Assistive technology and universal design for learning: Two sides of the same coin. In Edyburn, D. L., Higgins, K., & Boone, R. (eds.). *Handbook of special education technology research and practice* (pp. 507–18). Knowledge by Design.

Tar Heel Reader. (n.d.). Accessing Tar Heel Reader. https://tarheelreader.org/accessing-tar-heel-reader/.

University of Nebraska–Lincoln. (n.d.). Creating inclusive spaces: Safe space, brave space, allies and advocates. http://involved.unl.edu/inclusive-spaces.

Vizzle. (2020). Individualized online learning for special education. https://home.govizzle.com/.

Zabala, J. (2005). *Using the SETT framework to level the learning field for students with disabilities.* https://zabala.com/uploads/Zabala_SETT_Level ing_the_Learning_Field.pdf.

Chapter 8

Visual and Auditory Production

Lin Carver and Lauren Pantoja

It was a highly anticipated day in Mr. Lucas's eighth-grade history class. Students clamored through the door—their excitement palpable. This was the third day of sharing projects from their recent unit on the events that led to the American Revolution. Mr. Lucas had randomly drawn the events and assigned them to groups of three to four students. They worked on their projects for three days. All presentations were expected to include the same elements—who, what, when, where, why, and how the event contributed to the road to the revolution. Students were given the option of audio, video, or graphic presentations for their content, and specific programs were strongly recommended. The first two presentations were remarkably good; the time small groups spent collaborating and planning was used appropriately. The bar was set high and he looked forward to today's presentation as much as the students.

Two days ago, the first presentation had been a video about the Stamp Act; it had looked incredibly professional. The students even began with a short clip about expected audience behavior, which included silencing cell phones and no side conversations. The presenting group served popcorn and drinks. At the end of the presentation, Mr. Lucas had asked the class to summarize what they learned, and their recall was impressive. The second presentation described the Townshend Acts. The students had created a black and white comic book, had the audience read it aloud in small groups, and ended with a student-generated Kahoot quiz competition. Honestly,

Mr. Lucas was really proud, and if he were insecure about his instructional practices, these presentations would have intimidated him—they were fabulous! Today's group had opted for a rap; their topic was the Boston Massacre. He quieted the class and sat back as four students, Julio, Omar, Marcus, and Jana, made their way to the front of the classroom. All three boys wore homemade tricorn hats, Marcus carried a crazy lobster hat to represent the British Lobsterbacks, and Jana, the only girl in the group, wore an apron and shawl. They each had a sign around their neck: narrator, Ebenezer, Chris Seider, and Ebenezer's wife. Marcus put his lobster hat off to the side, and they all posed. The room was silent for about thirty seconds, a beat began to play from the back of the room, and then Julio began to rap.

In 1770 Boston was tense,
2000 British soldiers from the other side of the political fence
occupied Boston amidst 16,000 colonists
the result was practically a national apocalypse.

He then turned and faced the wall and Omar began:

Brawling and skirmishes took place daily
brought about by unhappy colonists mainly.
They protested taxes and vandalized stores
that sold supplies to soldiers from the other shore.

He then turned and faced the wall and Marcus chimed:

On the 22nd of February, Patriots attacked
the store of a Loyalist and it had a big impact.
It helped pave the way for the American Revolution
because the colonists were fed up with endless persecution.

Marcus turned and Jana began:

Ebenezer Richardson, who lived near the store,
tried to break up the crowd that was knockin' down the door.
He fired his gun through the window of his house. (The student
  wearing the Ebenezer sign lifted his hands and mimicked shooting
  a Brown Bess rifle.)

"What are you thinking!?!" Jana looked at the audience and said, "I'm his spouse." (She pointed to her sign.)
Eleven-year-old, Chris Seider, was killed by the shot. (The student wearing the Seider sign, fell to the ground.)
This put Richardson in a pretty bad spot.

The whole group stood, turned to the audience, and in unison rapped the chorus:

In 1770 Boston was tense,
2000 British soldiers from the other side of the political fence
occupied Boston amidst 16,000 colonists
the result was practically a national apocalypse.

The class clapped, hooted, and went wild. This was only the first act and Mr. Lucas could not wait to see what came next. He was going to have to up his instructional game; these students were killing it!

MULTISENSORY PRODUCTION

Technology integration is frequently assumed to mean that the teacher is allowing the students to use technology in the classroom. Frequently, this is evidenced in the form of each classroom within the school or district using a digital program that the district has purchased to help students master specific content standards. Often programs like iReady and Achieve 3000 are identified by districts and so these are perceived by these teachers as the pinnacle of technology integration in the classroom. When teachers in these schools talk about technology integration, the district-purchased skill-building programs are the methods that are discussed.

These programs do allow learners to interact with technology to demonstrate their learning, but they do not allow learners to create or produce knowledge to be shared with others. Learning is more than just identifying the correct answer. Learning is a multistep process. Learners must attend to the content to be mastered. Then they must form an understanding of the material through creating or identifying relationships among the ideas to be understood. Students then need to relate these new ideas to their prior knowledge.

Content creation or production allows for all of these processes to occur (Seifert, 1993).

When students take on the role of technology producers, digital integration looks different and has a different purpose than simply the use of district-purchased programs to support curriculum instruction. In the role of a technology producer, learners become scholars, creators, researchers, performers, designers, innovators, authors, and problem solvers. These roles may be evidenced differently in each content classroom. However, instead of just creating responses that are then submitted to or evaluated by the teacher, these producers are able to share their perspectives and analyses with their peers and colleagues as they contribute to knowledge construction within their classroom community (Bruff, 2013).

VISUAL PRODUCTION

We live in a visual society where learners are more attracted to visual media than traditional print texts (College Basics, 2019). Many learners tend to remember a greater percentage of what they see as compared to the percentage of what they hear. Presenting information in the form of visuals or graphics not only helps learners to understand the information, but it can also improve their learning by up to 400 percent (Emma, 2018). PowerPoints, although they often contain pictures, are generally text-based, so they do not support the acquisition of content as effectively as a visual format would. Medina (2018) determined that when students hear information, they will remember about 10 percent of it three days later while after the same time period learners will remember approximately 65 percent of the information from a picture. Shabiralyani et al. (2015) determined that visuals clarified content, enhanced vocabulary, and increased motivation.

Infographics, an effective way to share information, are visual representations that aim to make the data or content easily understandable since 90 percent of information that the brain receives and processes is visual. Pant (2015) indicated that the brain is able to process images 60,000 times faster than it can process written text and that 93 percent of all human communication is visual.

Infographics only minimally use text and are useful for displaying data, explaining concepts, simplifying presentations, mapping relationships, showing trends, and providing essential insights. The goal of infographics is to simplify large data sets by providing a high-level view and making the information easier to understand at first glance. They help to convey data in a compact and shareable form (Icons8Blog, n.d.). When students create infographics, the process helps them to think critically about the topic, logically organize the information, and display their understanding in various ways (Easelly, n.d.).

Many different programs are available for creating infographics; some of these are Canva, Venngage, and Piktochart. Most infographic programs include a variety of templates, fonts, and icons in a user-friendly drag and drop format. Canva is a platform with over one million images, fonts, icons, charts, graphs, and illustrations. Projects can be downloaded, but the program does not allow for videos or animated features (Walgrove, 2016). Venngage offers a variety of templates, some of which are free and some of which are available for an additional fee, organized by different types: statistical, informational, comparison, and geographic. Using this program creation is free, but you are limited to five infographics in your library. You can snip and save the infographics you create, but Venngage charges to export them from the program itself (Walgrove, 2016). The Piktochart program offers an additional feature. It allows you to import data or survey results from other sources and will allow you to embed videos. With this particular program, however, many of the templates are only available with the paid version (Walgrove, 2016).

But infographics are not the only option for visually conveying information. Comics appeal to learners of all ages and are another popular form that uses pictures with only small amounts of textual support in a sequential format. Comics can be a single frame, multiple frames, comic books, or even full-length graphic novels (College Basics, 2019). Many apps and websites for creating comics can be used within the classroom.

Kindergarten and first-grade learners will find the Draw and Tell by Duck, Duck, Moose app an effective springboard for drawing, coloring, and storytelling. Learners design or arrange a scene and then record a story to go along with the picture. The app will save the story, but once recorded, it cannot be added to or changed (Villamagna, 2012a). This same age group might enjoy the Superhero

Comic Book Maker. The app is a little more complicated, so students might need more teacher support. On-screen stickers can be used to add onomatopoeia words. Images cannot be changed or moved while recording the story, so the program construction might somewhat limit creativity (Villamagna, 2012b).

For students who are already able to read, Pixton, Make Beliefs Comix or Comic Life might be better choices for creating content-related comics. With the Pixton program, teachers create a classroom site and learners use a code to enter that site to create content-area cartoons. Using this program, students can add artwork, background, and text bubbles in addition to determining the number of frames and the page layout. Functions for sharing work and adding multimedia are easy to use, but the program only has limited potential for enabling students to use original artwork (VanderBorght, 2016). Make Beliefs Comix can be accessed through either the website or an app. Learners have options of adding dialogue, backgrounds, color, and objects. The items within the program can be scaled, flipped, or moved to allow for a better fit within the comic frame. The finished comic strip can be saved locally, printed, or emailed. Teachers should be aware that navigation within the program is not always smooth and original artwork cannot be used (Evenson, 2017). The Comic Life program contains subject-area templates that can be personalized for language arts, science, or social studies. Learners can use the drag and drop editor to arrange stock images or original pictures they have drawn. The program, although engaging, tends to be more time intensive than the other two programs discussed (Wisneski, 2019).

Word clouds are another option for visually displaying word-based qualitative data. Teachers might encourage students to use word clouds to display the most important words about a topic, responses to survey questions, or the most frequent themes in journal entries. Word clouds present a fast, low-cost alternative for students to analyze and share textual information. Word cloud programs assign font point sizes based upon the frequency of a word within the text; the more frequent the word, the larger it appears in the word cloud. However, the length of the word, the color, and the white space around it can make a word look more or less important in relation to the other words in the cloud (Vision Critical, 2012).

Many programs are available; however, three of the most commonly used programs are ABCYa! Word Clouds, Wordle, and Free online Wordcloud Generator. ABCYa! Word Clouds is a program that would be particularly appropriate for younger students because of its ease of use. Students paste the text into the box. The program creates the word cloud, and then the students adjust the font style, color, and layout of the text. The created word cloud can either be printed or saved. Wordle operates in much the same way. It is an easy-to-use tool for making word clouds by pasting a text into a text box and then choosing the font, color, and layout. It is easy to share the word cloud on the screen; however, several steps are required to share the file with others (Gannon, 2013). The versatility of Free Online Wordcloud Generator is particularly attractive since it can be used with any browser. Students paste their text into the text box and then design the word cloud by choosing the size, shape, flatness, theme, color, and font for their particular word cloud. Word clouds generated by this program can be arranged in a recognizable shape like an apple or a heart (Pappas, 2013).

AUDITORY PRODUCTION

Products created using audio components can be particularly effective for supporting auditory learners who want to share their ideas with their peers. Learners who prefer this format can easily comprehend and remember information that is presented through listening and speaking (Emma, 2018). Sometimes the auditory information is presented with an accompanying visual component. Flipgrid and Voki both fit into this category. They are programs where teachers or students can facilitate class discussions and content sharing. Although there are both auditory and visual components, generally the meaning is carried by the auditory portion of the program. In Flipgrid, each grid is a message board where the topic question is posed and fifteen-second to ten-minute responses are posted in the tiled grid display. Topics can be presented as text, images, videos, emojis, or attachments. Because video responses are customized, learners need to plan and create clearly expressed responses. However, a response can be recorded as many times as needed until the student is pleased with the content and presentation. The social media aspect of the Flipgrid could distract learners from the academic purpose of the assignment (Powers, 2018). Voki is a collection of customizable speaking avatars ranging from historic figures, cartoons, animals, or even yourself, which can be used to convey sixty to ninety minutes of content information generated by phone, microphone, or text-to-speech recording (Antonacci et al., 2014).

Learners might be interested in creating longer audio presentations without an accompanying video recording than are possible in Flipgrid. Students can use various options for creating audio recordings. Three they may want to explore are SpeakPipe, Voice Spice, or Anchor. SpeakPipe, which is compatible with both android and iOS devices, allows recordings to be saved for free, but a microphone or other input device is needed. Voice Spice Recorder has the ability to record voice, but it can also convert the recorded voice to other funny voices, such as birds, animal voices, or even the devil's voice. For this program, a microphone and a flash plugged browser are needed. Voice Spice Recorder is great for adding variety to recorded presentations (Cash, 2019). Anchor has a podcast-making app that would be effective for creating an audio project. The app allows for free unlimited recording, editing, and hosting for up to a 250 MB sized file. The program clearly records the ranges of the spoken voice, but it is not as effective for the highest and lowest frequencies of music (Boudreau, 2020).

A large part of the culture of today's youth includes hip-hop and rap. Rap involves words, which are rhyming or poetic, and hip-hop involves the music or beat. Music is a universal language and is key to promoting learning. Think of the wildly popular Broadway musical, *Hamilton*. This blockbuster is a hip-hop, rapping history lesson about the events in the life of one of the Founding Fathers of the United States, Alexander Hamilton. Lin Manuel, author and star of the musical, worked with two nonprofit organizations in New York City to bring 20,000, eleventh graders to not just see the play but also to "entice each of them to interpret original documents from the founding of our country and create their own artistic interpretation of a historical moment" (Strauss, 2016, para. 8). A New York City after-school program, Fresh Prep, uses rap to help students who have failed the NY Regents Exam. In this program, students learn the content of a text by listening, memorizing, and performing hip-hop songs to help them pass the test (Could Rap Music Actually, 2015). No matter what the content, the possibilities for using hip-hop and rap to support learning are endless. Flocabulary (2020) is an educational hip-hop and rap digital program that includes videos along with printable and interactive activities to support topics of learning in every content. One feature of the program is the Lyric Lab. The Lyric Lab is an interactive writing tool that supports students in writing their own academic rhyming raps. This tool includes a notes section to collect facts on the topic, a list of words associated with the topic, assistance with rhyming words for any word selected, the definition and the part of speech of words, and syllable tracking for lines of text to support the flow of the rhyme. Once finished, you can also export your rap as a PDF. A variety of beats are available to perform the rap (Flocabulary, 2020). To save the oral presentation of the rap, an additional recording tool will be needed. AutoRap by SMULE is a hip-hop, rap-creating application that is similar to karaoke and can be used on an iPad or iPhone. AutoRap will take any words that students record on the app and transform them into a rhythm. There is also a variety of original and popular beats from which you can choose (Harris, 2012). Educators should monitor the use of AutoRap because students can be challenged to rap by unknown persons over the Internet, and many of the published raps have mature language and content (SaferKid, 2016). However, if teachers supervise the recording, the rap can be emailed and safely listened to outside the application.

QUESTION/REVIEW PRODUCTION

Stock (2019) stressed the importance of allowing students to teach others the information to be mastered. She indicated that *learning by teaching* is a newer strategy of which more teachers should take advantage. This is a particularly important principle when preparing students for assessments. Teachers could prepare review questions, but it is even more effective if students take ownership of this activity and prepare the review for their peers. Many programs are available to support this activity. Some of the most frequently used are Poll Everywhere, Quizizz, Socrative, and Survey Monkey. Poll Everywhere is a student-response tool that encourages whole-class participation through surveys, polls, and discussion boards. Students can construct polls to collect peer responses or questions for content review. The setup is quick and provides for immediate feedback. Because each poll must be reset individually, the design is somewhat outdated (Rogowski, 2019b). Quizizz is compatible with most operating systems and is a game show-style quiz tool. Teachers must create an account, but students do not have to create one. It is a multiple-choice-style quiz tool that allows for some customization. However, when using touch screens, students can easily tap on the wrong choice (Bindel, 2018). Socrative is an interactive Web-based student response system that uses polls and quizzes. Students get a room code where they can respond to quizzes, quick questions, and exit slips through multiple-choice, true/false, and one-sentence responses. Learners receive instant feedback but tracking student data over time is more difficult with this system (Rogowski, 2018a). Survey Monkey allows students to create and distribute a ten-question survey for free. Responses can be formatted in Likert scales, multiple-choice, multiple responses, or short answers.

PORTFOLIOS PRODUCTION

Portfolios have begun to be used as a way to assess students' progress and performance. Originally, portfolios were used to display artist's work (Moya & O'Malley, 1994) and later this purpose was extended to showcase experiential learning (Farr & Tone, 1998). This practice has been further expanded to include educational portfolios in various content areas (Melles, 2009). Portfolios enable students to monitor, evaluate, and reflect on their learning (Wang & Chang, 2011). There are various types of portfolios that can be used in the K–12 setting. A working portfolio contains items the student is currently working on. A display portfolio showcases samples of the student's best work. An assessment portfolio demonstrates how the student has met specific standards or learning goals. Sometimes products cannot be easily displayed or appropriately captured in a paper format. A digital portfolio allows for various types of artifacts to be included. Using hyperlinks to connect sections is an advantage of an electronic portfolio (Brown, 2011).

Seesaw is digital portfolio that can house videos, photos, text, images, files, and drawings. Teachers can provide feedback, and projects can be shared with families and peers as well. The student and the teacher interfaces are easy to use and provide many suggestions.

However, the skills and standards need to be entered manually (Rogowski, 2018b). Evernote is a popular cloud-based app for creating digital portfolios for secondary students. Photos, notes, audio, and searchable entries can be included in the portfolio. The program allows for cross-device syncing, voice recording, collaboration, and includes markup features. The tagging and notebook features help to keep it organized. Teachers should be aware that there is no way to password-protect the desktop version and that accessibility features are somewhat limited (Rogowski, 2019a).

Edmodo is a free Facebook-like learning management platform that allows for social media interactions and combines three purposes: displaying classroom content, providing safe communication, and allowing for assessment. Users can share documents, links, videos, and images using the drag-and-drop feature, which can be integrated with Google and Microsoft accounts. The busy interface and ads might present challenges (Rogowski, 2020). Live Binders is a program that is more appropriate for secondary learners. Documents, websites, and media can be uploaded to the tabs within each binder, which can be arranged with a table of contents. The free version includes ten binders and limited storage, but the tool has limited visual appeal (Gorrell, 2017).

CONCLUSION

Learning is a multistep process that occurs when students construct or identify relationships among ideas and when they connect new knowledge to what they know. When students are taking what they have learned and creating or producing a product, they are employing these processes (Seifert, 1993). There is an abundance of digital tools that can be used by students to creatively demonstrate learning.

Why use digital tools to demonstrate learning? Digital resources motivate students and promote critical thinking and creativity using multisensory skills with an array of creative possibilities. Predominantly, visual resources for demonstrating learning include digitally created infographics, pictures and picture books, word clouds, and single or multiple frame comics. For students who prefer primarily auditory production tools that are generated by speaking, there are products with accompanying visual components, but the learning is primarily demonstrated auditorily. These products could be a video of the learner speaking or a talking avatar. Strictly audio products can also be created via podcasts, voice recorder apps, and apps for producing hip-hop and rap. Students can create questions for their peers to demonstrate learning using a variety of digital apps for generating games, polls, or quizzes. Portfolios to highlight a student's course accomplishments are a performance evaluation tool that encourages students to evaluate and reflect on their own learning. There are a number of digital portfolios available for students to house their work making the process easily accessible for reflection, feedback, and collaboration.

The verb "create" is one of the peak performance tasks on learning taxonomies for good reason. When students create products to demonstrate understanding, we support them in the synthesis and internalization of their learning. Technology producers are prepared for the twenty-first-century challenges by becoming scholars, creators, researchers, performers, designers, innovators, authors, and problem solvers. Motivate and engage our learners with technological production and our students' cognitive development will soar.

REFLECT AND APPLY ACTIVITIES

8.1. Using one type of visual production software described in this chapter that you have not previously used, develop a visual you could use to teach others about various types they could use in their instruction. Identify at least four different types.
8.2. Using one type of questioning or review software discussed in this chapter that you have not used previously, create a set of questions related to a topic you would present to others.

REFERENCES

Antonacci, P., O'Callaghan, C. M., & Berkowitz, E. (2015). *Developing content area literacy: 40 strategies for middle and secondary classrooms* (2nd ed.). Sage.
Bindel, A. (2018, September). Quizizz. Common Sense Education. https://www.commonsense.org/education/website/quizizz.

Boudreau, M. (2020, February). Anchor review: Is it worth using Anchor to make a podcast? The Podcast Host. https://www.thepodcasthost.com/planning/using-anchor-to-make-a-podcast/.

Brown, M. D. (2011). Using technology: Electronic portfolios in the K–12 classroom. Education World. https://www.educationworld.com/a_tech/tech/tech111.shtml.

Bruff, D. (2013, September). Students as producers: An introduction. Center for Teaching Vanderbilt University. https://cft.vanderbilt.edu/2013/09/students-as-producers-an-introduction/.

Cash, A. (2019, August). Top 10 free audio recorder online services. Aimersoft. https://www.aimersoft.com/record-music/audio-recorder-online.html.

College Basics. (2019). The benefits of comics in student learning. Admission News. https://www.collegebasics.com/blog/benefits-of-comics/.

Could rap music actually be a valuable asset in the classroom? (2015, November 16). *Think Fun.* http://info.thinkfun.com/stem-education/could-rap-music-actually-be-a-valuable-asset-in-the-classroom.

Easelly. (n.d.) Show, don't tell. Author. https://www.easel.ly/blog/infographics-effective-classroom/.

Emma. (2018, January). How to use technology for different learning styles. Learn Safe. https://learnsafe.com/how-to-use-technology-for-different-learning-styles/.

Evenson, F. (2017, December). Make beliefs comix. Common Sense Education. https://www.commonsense.org/education/website/make-beliefs-comix.

Farr, R. & Tone, B. (1998). *Portfolio and performance assessment: Helping students evaluate their progress as readers and writers.* Harcourt Brace.

Flocabulary. (2020). engaging lessons per every subject. https://flexabilatiy.com/how-it-works/

Gannon, V. (2013, May). Wordle. Common Senses Education. https://www.commonsense.org/education/website/wordle.

Gorrell, D. (2017, February). LiveBinders. Common Sense Education. https://www.commonsense.org/education/website/livebinders.

Harris, C. (2012, September 6). "A" is for app. *Huffpost.* https://www.huffpost.com/entry/autorap-app_b_1854999.

Icons8Blog. (n.d.). What is an infographic: Types, examples, tips. https://icons8.com/articles/what-is-an-infographic/.

Medina, J. (2018). Brain rules. http://www.brainrules.net/vision.

Melles, G. (2009). Teaching and evaluation of critical appraisal skills to post-graduate ESL engineering students. *Innovations in Education and Teaching International, 46*(2), 161–70. doi:10.1080/14703290902843810.

Moya, S. S. & O'Malley, M. (1994). A portfolio assessment model for ESL. *Journal of Educational Issues of Language Minority Students, 13*, 13–36.

Pant, R. (2015, January). Visual marketing: A picture's worth 60,000 words. Business 2 Community. https://www.business2community.com/

digital-marketing/visual-marketing-pictures-worth-60000-words-01126256#e7IpHbm5JO6p7UJx.99.

Pappas, C. (2013, November). The 8 best free word cloud creation tools for teachers. eLearning Industry. https://elearningindustry.com/the-8-best-free-word-cloud-creation-tools-for-teachers.

Powers, M. (2018, November). Flipgrid. Common Sense Education. https://www.commonsense.org/education/website/flipgrid.

Rogowski, M. (2018a, October). Socrative. Common Sense Education. https://www.commonsense.org/education/website/socrative.

Rogowski, M. (2018b, October). Seesaw: The learning journal. Common Sense Education. https://www.commonsense.org/education/app/seesaw-the-learning-journal.

Rogowski, M. (2019a, April). Evernote. Common Sense Education. https://www.commonsense.org/education/app/evernote.

Rogowski, M. (2019b, November). Poll everywhere. Common Sense Education. https://www.commonsense.org/education/website/poll-everywhere.

Rogowski, M. (2020, April). Edmodo. Common Sense Education. https://www.commonsense.org/education/website/edmodo.

SaferKid. (2016). App Rating AutoRap by Smule. https://www.saferkid.com/app-reviews-for-parents/autorap-by-smule.

Seifert, T. (1993, Fall). Learning strategies in the classroom. https://www.mun.ca/educ/faculty/mwatch/vol2/seifert.html.

Shabiralyani, G., Hasan, S. K., Hamad, N., & Iqbal, N. (2015). Impact of visual aids in enhancing the learning process case research: District Dera Ghazi Khan. *Journal of Education and Practice, 6*(19), 226–33. https://files.eric.ed.gov/fulltext/EJ1079541.pdf.

Stock, E. (2019, January). Want students to remember what they learn? Have them teach it. EdSurge. https://www.edsurge.com/news/2019-01-24-want-students-to-remember-what-they-learn-have-them-teach-it.

Strauss, V. (2016, June 28). The unusual way Broadway's "Hamilton" is teaching U.S. history to kids. *The Washington Post.* https://www.washingtonpost.com/news/answer-sheet/wp/2016/06/28/the-unusual-way-broadways-hamilton-is-teaching-american-history-to-kids/.

VanderBorght, M. (2016, November). Pixton. Common Sense Education. https://www.commonsense.org/education/website/pixton.

Villamagna, D. (2012a, August). Draw and tell HD by Duck Moose. Common Sense Education. https://www.commonsense.org/education/app/draw-and-tell-hd-by-duck-duck-moose.

Villamagna, D. (2012b, August). Superhero comic book maker. Common Sense Education. https://www.commonsense.org/education/app/superhero-comic-book-maker.

Vision Critical. (2012, August). Clouds as visualization. Author. https://www.visioncritical.com/blog/pros-and-cons-word-clouds-visualizations.

Walgrove, A. (2016, September). The pros, cons, and costs of the top 5 DIY infographic tools. The Freelancer. https://contently.net/2016/09/01/resources/tools/apps/pros-cons-costs-top-5-diy-infographic-tools/.

Wang, L. J. & Chang, H. F. (2011, July–September). Improve oral training: The method of innovation assessment on English speaking performance. *International Journal of Distance of Education Technologies*, *9*(3), http://dx.doi.org.saintleo.idm.oclc.org/10.4018/jdet.2011070105.

Wisneski, S. (2019, October). Comic Life. Common Sense Education. https://www.commonsense.org/education/website/comic-life.

Chapter 9

Enhancing Social and Emotional Learning through Technology

Lin Carver and Lauren Pantoja

Mrs. Kilpatrick looked around her sixth-grade language arts classroom. She remembered back to the beginning of the school year when her students had sat silently in small cliques around her room hesitant to interact with students they did not know. Now they were a much more integrated group who were willing to work and learn together.

At the beginning of the school year, in an attempt to support the transition to middle school and further develop her students' social and emotional skills, Mrs. Kilpatrick had introduced her students to the Middle School Confidential program. The graphic novels on which the program is based appealed to her students and they had read them eagerly. After reading, individually or in small groups, the students had examined how to help the characters solve their problems. The beginning sections and discussions about teasing and body image had been particularly appropriate for her middle school students and were a great way to start the year.

Mrs. Kilpatrick was particularly pleased with the way the app had helped her students expand their reading comprehension skills and inferential thinking. She was thrilled that the program could also be used to help develop writing skills and that these were not overlooked. In the program, students compose emails to the story characters expressing their ideas and sharing their feelings about various topics. This was a great opportunity to help her students develop their written expression. The program helped her address important

133

academic skills and helped her students develop self-confidence by exploring school-related social experiences such as handling bullying, building friendships, and promoting a healthy classroom culture.

SOCIAL/EMOTIONAL RESOURCES

The goal of our K–12 educational system is to increase students' learning. Because of the emphasis on grade-level standards, instruction tends to focus on academic concerns; however, learning is a social activity (Vygotsky, 1978), so the development of social and emotional competencies is equally important (Zins et al., 2004). Brenner and Salovey (1997) found that emotion aids intelligence and shapes thinking by increasing motivation and attention. Sharma et al. (2009) determined that emotions are culturally and socially constructed; however, this development is further impacted by gender differences (Bar-On, 2004). Bar-On (2004) found that generally females have more fully developed interpersonal skills, self-awareness, and social responsibility while males demonstrated higher levels of intrapersonal skills, emotional management, and self-regard.

The Collaborative for Academic, Social, and Emotional Learning (CASEL) provides the most frequently used definition for social and emotional learning (SEL). They define SEL as the "process through which children and adults understand and manage emotions, set and achieve positive goals, feel and show empathy for others, establish and maintain positive relationships, and make responsible decisions" (CASEL, 2020a, para. 1). These skills include five related competencies: self-awareness, self-management, social awareness, relationship skills, and responsible decision-making (Krause, 2019).

The competency of self-awareness includes the understanding of emotions, personal identity, goals, and values. These components are developed through using a positive mindset, self-efficacy, and optimism to accurately assess personal strengths and limitations. Self-aware students understand the links between personal and sociocultural identities and recognize the interconnections between thoughts, feelings, and actions. The competency of self-management encompasses the skills and attitudes that regulate emotions and behaviors. It is evidenced in the ability to achieve personal and educational goals through delaying gratification, managing stress, controlling impulses, and persevering through personal and group-level challenges. The competency of social awareness involves the ability to adopt other's perspectives and to feel compassion or empathy for those from the same or different backgrounds and cultures. Learners can demonstrate the ability to identify community, school, and family resources and understand social norms for behavior in diverse settings. The relationship competency skills are evidenced by the ability to establish and maintain healthy and rewarding relationships, and to navigate settings with differing social norms and demands. Relationship competency skills require appropriately developed clear communication, active listening, cooperation, resisting inappropriate social pressures, negotiating conflict constructively, and the ability to know when to seek help. The last competency, responsible decision-making, encompasses the knowledge, skills, and attitudes needed to make caring, constructive choices about behavior and social interactions in diverse settings by critically examining ethical standards, safety concerns, and behavioral norms affecting the health and well-being of others (Jager et al., 2018).

SOCIAL EMOTIONAL CONCERNS

K–12 students face many issues related to social emotional and mental health concerns. These mental health concerns cross gender, racial, and socioeconomic lines. A survey of teens across demographic groups revealed that mental health concerns were a significant issue in their community (Horowitz & Graf, 2019). With the current increase in racially motivated violence and unrest, the impact and benefits of SEL instruction are being investigated even more extensively.

A meta-analysis of 213 studies (Durlak et al., 2011) indicated that involving students in SEL instruction resulted in increased academic achievement. Based on the data collected from 270,000 students, the researchers determined that those students who participated in evidence-based SEL programs showed an 11 percent point gain in academic achievement.

However, this is not the only benefit of SEL programs. Durlak and Mahoney (2019) compared performance between students enrolled in SEL programs and those not enrolled in these programs and determined the following for students enrolled in SEL programs: 24 percent more of these students demonstrated improved social behaviors and lower levels of distress; 23 percent experienced improved attitudes about themselves, others, and school; and 22 percent demonstrated fewer conduct problems, which resulted in improved classroom behavior. Research also determined that students enrolled in SEL programs experienced decreases in dropout rates, drug use, teen pregnancy, mental health problems, and criminal behavior (CASEL, 2020b).

Stress is a significant concern for our youth, no matter which gender, race, or socioeconomic level. This was particularly evident in the teen population. Survey results indicated that most teens (61 percent) felt a lot of pressure to get good grades, and another 27 percent said they felt some pressure in this area (Horowitz & Graf, 2019).

The CASEL core SEL competencies, in addition to addressing the needs of all students, are also included in programs and practices that support the development of these competencies in an attempt to promote educational equity (Jager et al., 2018). Using SEL competencies to promote the optimal development of all students, especially preK–12 students who have historically been underserved, can be a complex and long-term undertaking. But this effort is one that will benefit all learners.

CULTURALLY RESPONSIVE TEACHING

Culturally responsive teaching is an approach to instruction that makes connections to what students learn and their life experiences, language, and culture (Understood, 2020). It can also support the development of diverse students' social and emotional skills. "In culturally responsive pedagogy, the classroom is a critical container for empowering marginalized students. It serves as a space that reflects the values of trust, partnership, and academic mindset that are at its core" (Hammond, 2015, p. 143). Today's educators, who are consciously embedding SEL and culturally responsive teaching, want to be certain that their instructional practices are responsive to and equitable for all students including those who have historically been marginalized. Some students' lives have been impacted by external, discriminatory practices, and these students may need social and emotional support to counteract these forces (Seider & Graves, 2020). In order to help culturally diverse students develop social and emotional competencies, it is important that educators understand these students' cultures (Torres, 2019). It would be challenging, and perhaps impossible, for social-emotional learning to occur without that understanding. Culturally responsive teaching not only benefits diverse students in the classroom, it also enhances the development of social awareness for all students by encouraging understanding of perspectives and experiences of individuals from different backgrounds and cultures.

All learning begins with oral language. Memory strategies associated with these oral language skills include rhythm, music, poetic recitations, and riddles. Many games apply cultural tools from oral traditions, which include repetition, problem-solving, and making connections. Teachers' use of collaboration brings in the social aspect associated with the oral language dimension and helps to build communication skills. Finally, cultural experiences are rife with stories; when learning is turned into a story, the brain makes connections that facilitate understanding (Hammond, 2015). To help learners succeed, teachers can use the learner's culture, gender, experiences, and frames of reference to increase learning (Rhodes & Schmidt, 2018).

BENEFITS OF SOCIAL-EMOTIONAL LEARNING

Although there are costs involved with every new program, the benefits of incorporating SEL programs have been investigated. Belfield et al.'s (2015) research of six SEL programs found that for every dollar invested in the program there was an economic return of $11. Although the researchers were not able to calculate the full economic value of SEL programs, since education in substance abuse, aggression, and attitudes are difficult to directly measure in a financial way, shadow prices were used in this research to evaluate the financial impact of SEL programs. Three types of benefits were analyzed in this study. First, the immediate benefits were considered. These are the ones that occur as the SEL program is being delivered. Second, post-intervention benefits that occur after the intervention has been delivered but while the participants are still in school were calculated. Third, the post-intervention benefits that occur during adulthood after the participants have left school were considered.

Employers have always attempted to recruit employees with high levels of professional skills, prior experience, technical skills, and/or academic achievement. However, in addition, surveys determined that employers regarded the social emotional skills of collaboration, critical thinking, ethical and social responsibility, professionalism, and effective communication even more highly (McGraw-Hill Education, 2017). These skills need to be explicitly taught, beginning in preschool and continuing through higher education (Oberle et al., 2016). This explicit instruction, when delivered over time, has been shown to lead to long-term benefits during school, such as increases in academic engagement and decreases in bullying and school suspensions. These benefits were found to extend into early adulthood. SEL-proficient individuals tended to have higher levels of mental well-being, greater success in higher education and the workplace, and higher income levels than their less-proficient peers (Oberle et al., 2016). The need for enhanced SEL has been acknowledged through federal legislation mandating the measurement of social and emotional growth, and throughout the world, as organizations, such as the Organization for Economic Cooperation and Development, integrate the competencies into their agendas (Oberle et al., 2016).

The impact of these social emotional skills, sometimes labeled as "soft skills," have often been overlooked in the educational technology area in favor of the specific thinking and coding skills that are more easily measured and used for assessing academic ability and growth. The relationship between social and emotional skills and technology skills is being reevaluated as we discover their interreliance in terms of long-term measures of success. Soft skills help build important qualities such as attention, motivation, and a growth mindset, which are among the many attributes that students can cultivate through their use of technology.

Rapid advances in technological capabilities have led to breakthroughs in everything from portability, data analytics, and communication methods. As a result of the growing interest in SEL and its role in education and the workplace, SEL and available technologies continue to evolve. The possibility of using technology to enhance

SEL is no longer a dream for the future, but it is a growing reality for today's learners. Technology education is becoming an important component in the K–12 educational experiences. Students are learning to code, experiencing mixed media realities, visiting virtual worlds, and exploring apps and extensions. They are being immersed into technology that brings learning to life. But the issue educators face is can SEL and technology education actually be combined?

Technology development has focused on enhancing students' voices, individual expression, visible learning, oral language, and SEL, all important components in SEL and culturally responsive teaching. From Smiling Mind to Social Expression and Simple Better to Social Quest (just to name a few), EdTech producers are developing ways to include students' voices, foster wellness, and promote social learning across disciplines and cultures while providing accessibility for all. These are big visions, and the timing is ripe for expansion in this area.

Adobe, founded in 1982, focuses on the creation of multimedia, creativity software products, and digital marketing software. The company is well known for its Adobe Flash web software, Photoshop, Adobe Illustrator, Acrobat Reader, Adobe Creative Suite, and the Adobe Creative Cloud. All of these products have provided and expanded opportunities for students' expression and social learning, important components of SEL. Adobe Connect further builds on this ability by allowing for students' interactions in meetings, webinars, and virtual classrooms.

TECHNOLOGY AS A BRIDGE

Educators are realizing that technology can be a bridge, helping students and teachers to connect with each other no matter what the age of learners. Positive social and emotional development in the early years provides a critical foundation for lifelong development and learning. Head Start (2020) defines social development as a child's ability to create and sustain meaningful relationships with adults and other children. A survey of over 400 primary schools in England determined that providing SEL is an important concern. Forty-six percent of the primary schools indicated that SEL was their top priority while a further 49 percent believed it to be an important consideration alongside a number of other priorities (Grenier & Gross, 2020). Jones et al. (2015) in their research determined that social-emotional wellness evidenced by kindergarten students correlated with success up until the age of twenty-five. Consequently, beginning social emotional instruction early is an important consideration. Technology can be used to complement our efforts in helping students develop these social emotional skills (Zimmerman, 2018). The question for technology developers has become: How does SEL look when it's built into technology?

TECHNOLOGY FOR YOUNG CHILDREN

Many apps for developing social and emotional skills are appropriate for young children. For helping youngsters recognize, identify, and describe emotions, apps like ABA Flash Card Emotions, iLearn with Poko: Emotions, and Avokiddo Emotions might be interesting to explore (iGame Mom, 2020). The free app Breathe, Think, Do with Sesame takes youngsters a step further. It was developed to help young children ages two to five years of age learn methods for problem-solving, self-control, planning, and task persistence when faced with everyday challenges, rather than just focusing on identifying the emotion. Children can engage with activities in English or Spanish as they help the monsters calm down and develop a plan to overcome challenges (Sesame Street, 2020).

Smiling Mind is a free online program and app that is appropriate for children from preschool to teenagers to engage them in mindfulness, so they will pay closer attention to being in the moment with curiosity, open-mindedness, and without judgment (TeachThought Staff, 2020). The app includes short meditation sessions for different purposes, such as focusing on breathing, paying attention to their body, cultivating gratitude, connecting with curiosity, and listening mindfully. The app includes meditation sessions for four different age groups from three to eighteen. The modules vary for each age group, but they include topics such as empathy and kindness, mindful listening, awareness and sounds, and thoughts and feelings. Each module is composed of a variety of sessions (Smiling Mind, 2020).

TECHNOLOGY FOR SCHOOL-AGE STUDENTS

On the K–12 level, social-emotional learning technology is available in many different forms from apps to Web-based programs. Be Confident in Who You Are and Real Friends vs. the Other Kind are comic book apps with age-appropriate scenarios that present issues for the tween and teenage groups. These are role-play apps where teens help rebuild the community using social and emotional skills through interactions with various characters (iGame Mom, 2020). These digital resources can be used to help teachers integrate SEL into the classroom setting in ways that are meaningful and appropriate while providing teachers and students methods for measuring the effectiveness of SEL and their progress toward specific learning objectives. These software programs can analyze and adapt to students' behaviors, interpersonal skills, and progress to meet individual needs. Practicing social emotional skills through technology has proven to be especially beneficial to students with special needs, as it provides them with a less pressurized learning environment while giving them a sense of control over their own learning (W. N., 2019).

Another example of this union of technology and SEL is the SiLAS program. Using this software, students write a script for a social situation, such as working cooperatively with a classmate. The learners then record a real-time animated video acting out their script. All of this is achieved using video-game controllers and headset microphones, similar to those used in the students' favorite video games. Teachers monitor students' learning with pre- and post-assessments as well as rubrics based on the lesson objective. These programs provide students opportunities to practice with and further envision SEL skills in action (Center on Technology and Disability, 2020).

For students between eight and fourteen years of age who enjoy graphic novels, Middle School Confidential might be the perfect program. The program involves three app-based graphic novels with characters who help each other grapple with typical middle-school problems and self-doubt. It is a program to help learners develop self-confidence by exploring school-related social experiences such as handling bullying, building friendships, and promoting a healthy classroom culture. At the end of each chapter, there is a quiz related to the chapter topic that assesses what students would do in challenging situations. An extra bonus of this program is that players can email the characters in the story and discuss or share their feelings (Dussault, 2018).

TECHNOLOGY FOR TEENS

Social Express is a program designed to help teenagers understand emotions and handle social situations. Using interactive animated videos, the learner becomes the protagonist in many different scenes and determines the actions that will help to develop positive social interactions (Dussault, 2018). The program uses vignettes and additional materials to teach behavioral principles that include the comprehension of concepts, how these concepts are conveyed in social situations, and why these social conventions/expressions are important (Krach et al., 2020). The Social Express program includes over eighty-one webisodes that teach foundational skills for social-emotional learning that include, but are not limited to, conflict resolution, group participation, relationships, and self-management. Lessons support such topics as identifying feelings in others, developing coping strategies, learning how to start conversations, reading nonverbal social cues, or learning about the hidden rules in social situations (The Social Express, 2020).

Get Media L.I.T. is a Web-based learning platform for students in grades six through twelve. This comic-based program includes three focus areas: literacy, digital citizenship, and social-emotional learning. The "playlists" for social-emotional learning include a variety of topics such as "How do you show empathy in a machine-driven world?" and "How do you build self-confidence?" It also supports culturally responsive teaching with topics such as "What if I'm not What Media Says I Should Be?" Teachers guide their students through short lessons that spin off the comic library, which features a group of superheroes known as The Uncommons. Each lesson has three parts: Learn, which is the introduction to the concept or topic; Inquire, which focuses on critical thinking or analysis of the topic; and Transform, which is the application of the concept inside and outside of the classroom (Weird Enough Productions, 2020). According to Common Sense Education (2019), many of the comics pose complicated vignettes and the discussion questions require background knowledge and higher-order thinking that might be difficult for typical middle school students. The comics are authentic and the conversation starters are compelling, but the lessons do not seem to lead to a solid final product or differentiation. Any appropriate ancillary materials would be up to the teacher to provide (Common Sense Education, 2019). However, if the teacher's objective is to provide an engaging context for thoughtful, relevant conversations around current events impacting students in today's world, then Get Media L.I.T. is an excellent classroom resource.

TECHNOLOGY TO SUPPORT INDIVIDUAL LEARNING

A variety of apps are also available, which can be used to further individualize instruction in SEL and to develop a growth mindset. For those students who enjoy video games, Super Better is a great choice. Through making healthy choices, the players can "power up" within this self-regulated, self-paced app to reach individual goals. This free app can be used to plan homework, study, overcome anxiety, develop healthy habits, maintain a positive attitude, and develop better social and emotional skills. Because the app does not include adult direction, this program is best for learners who have good levels of self-control (Dussault, 2018).

Social Quest is an app that can be used to develop empathy, label feelings, understand perspectives, and enhance self-awareness. It was developed for students twelve years of age and older who struggle with expressing themselves or responding appropriately in particular social situations. In this app, the students are on a quest to find a positive way to problem-solve various real-world situations in a variety of locations—at home, in the community, and/or at school. Students earn rewards as they progress through the program (Social Quest, n.d.). An adult needs to determine if the students will be working on expressive or receptive language, but the students will need to create an avatar or character to begin their quests. There is instant feedback and long-term rewards to encourage engagement (Kemper, 2019).

TECHNOLOGY TO SUPPORT
CLASS LEARNING

Some programs or apps can be used to help entire classrooms work on social emotional skills rather than focusing on individual students' needs. Programs like Connect, GSuite, and Office365 are examples of technology that can be used to promote social-emotional learning with the entire class. Teachers can support differentiated learning by encouraging students to track and measure their own progress and assess their own learning. Using these tools, students are able to use teacher feedback to determine areas of personal struggle and growth in real time and, as a result, are provided with more intuitive, individualized learning experiences. Microsoft Office, for example, includes Fligrid and TEAMS. Flipgird is a digital, social learning program where educators create meeting places for students (grids) to discuss various topics. Students respond to the teacher's prompts and each other via video or voice (Flipgrid, 2020). Microsoft TEAMS is a videoconferencing tool with many additional features and integration options such as a whiteboard, screen share, embedded images, polls, and much more (Duffy, 2020). In addition, the ability to share documents, files, and presentation apps in Microsoft Office supports student collaboration. All of these tools can be used by teachers and students to help learners set and meet realistic, individual goals while supporting social skills through collaboration.

The app How Would You Feel If was developed for kindergarten through third-grade students. It includes colorful picture cards with accessible audio of the text that poses a variety of situations. The teacher selects the cards for the students to see and can print and even grade students' responses (Webber & Wise, 2020).

In 2017, the Kind Foundation launched a free online tool for six- to eleven-year-old children to connect classrooms across the globe. The goal of the program is to connect teachers and students, so they can see other communities and learn about the lives of others who are different from themselves. A classroom teacher begins by registering for the program and selecting a partner class. The teachers chat, share pictures and videos, and set up a schedule. Activities are then provided that encourage empathy, curiosity, and kindness. The activities involve three steps: prepare for your virtual meeting, interact with your partner classroom in a live virtual exchange, and finally reflect on the experience. Empatico, the publisher, provides the activities and includes information on the research behind their activities as well as the academic standards and the connection to twenty-first-century skills and social-emotional learning standards (Empatico, 2017).

Storyboard That is a browser-based storyboard creator where students begin by selecting the appearance of their storyboard. They choose from a variety of preloaded scenes and select their characters who they can personalize and pose. Speech bubbles and/or audio recordings can be added to create the storyline. Students determine the number of cells for the storyboard and can add various additional options, including using their own voice to record the story. Individual or collaborative original stories can be created that address social-emotional skills or address personal goals. The storyboards can be exported in many formats, including PowerPoint, Google Slides, or PDF files (Shedd, 2019). There are many creative ways that Storyboard That can be used to support SEL and students will definitely have fun being creative.

CONCLUSION

Numerous digital resources for promoting SEL with technology are available. The concept of learning around technology places emphasis on tools that support social practices, solutions, understandings, task-related talk, and prosocial behaviors (Goldsworthy, 2002). These tools and activities allow for structured tasks, problem-solving, and appropriate social interactions while supporting Kutnick's (1997) notion of planned joint actions through which learners work and discuss together as partners. It is evident that SEL can be fostered and developed through activities such as collaborative interaction, dialogue, reflection, problem-solving, and decision-making in face-to-face or online settings supported by digital tools such as networked computers, digital animations, learning management systems, discussion forums, mind-mapping tools, apps, and learning journals (Iaosanurak et al., 2015). Digital resources provide a solution for supporting SEL.

REFLECT AND APPLY ACTIVITIES

9.1. Consider the five CASEL competencies for social-emotional learning, self-awareness, self-management, social awareness, relationship skills, and responsible decision-making. Which of these competencies should be a priority for your students? Select a digital resource that can be used to address this competency either from one mentioned in this chapter or one that you have researched. Share your rationale for the competency you selected and explain how the digital resource can be used to support your students.

9.2. After reading this chapter, try one of the digital resources you have not previously used and explain how it could be used in your setting to support social-emotional learning for your learners.

REFERENCES

Belfield, C., Bowden, B., Klapp, A., Levin, H., Shand, R., & Zander, S. (2015). The economic value of social and emotional learning. http://blogs.edweek.org/edweek/rulesforengagement/SEL-Revised.pdf.

Bar-On, R. (2004). The Bar-On emotional quotient inventory (EQ-i): Rationale, description and summary of psychometric properties. In G. Geher (ed.), *Measuring emotional intelligence: Common ground and controversy* (pp. 115–46). Nova.

Brenner, E. M. & Salovey, P. (1997). Emotional regulation during childhood: Developmental, interpersonal, and individual considerations. In P. Salovey & D. J. Sluyter (eds.), *Emotional development and emotional intelligence: Educational implications* (pp. 168–95). HarperCollins.

CASEL. (2020a). What is SEL? https://casel.org/what-is-sel/.

CASEL. (2020b). SEL impact. https://casel.org/impact/.

Center on Technology and Disability. (2020). SILAS: Autism socialization training software. https://www.ctdinstitute.org/library/2018-01-03/silas-autism-socialization-training-software.

Durlak, J. & Mahoney, J. (2019, December). The practical benefits of an SEL program. https://casel.org/wp-content/uploads/2019/12/Practical-Benefits-of-SEL-Program.pdf.

Duffy, J. (2020, March 25). Microsoft teams review. *PC.* https://www.pcmag.com/reviews/microsoft-teams.

Durlak, J. Weissberg. R., Dymnick, A. Taylor, R., & Schellinger, K. (2011). The impact of enhancing students' social and emotional learning:

A meta-analysis of school-based universal interventions. *Child Development, 82*(1), 405–32. https://casel.org/wp-content/uploads/2016/01/meta-analysis-child-development-1.pdf.

Dussault, A. (2018, August). The 5 best social emotional learning apps for teachers. https://www.classcraft.com/blog/features/the-5-best-social-emotional-learning-apps-for-teachers/.

Empatico. (2017). *The KIND Foundation.* https://empatico.org/?gclid=CjwKCAjw0_T4BRBlEiwAwoEiAepQLpsT-8cqoGt9u_4lq9Jqte KyAgjUiY-Fodqrh-ACO6m0bXp5fRoC4OsQAvD_BwE.

Educators' Team at Understood. (2020). Culturally responsive teaching: What you need to know. *Understood.* https://www.understood.org/en/school-learning/for-educators/universal-design-for-learning/what-is-culturally-responsive-teaching.

Flipgrid. (2020). Empower every voice. https://info.flipgrid.com/.

Goldsworthy, R. (2002). Supporting the development of emotional intelligence through technology. *Computers in the Schools, 19*(1–2), 119–48. doi:10.1300/J025v19n01_10.

Grenier, J. & Gross, J. (2020). *Improving social and emotional learning in early years and primary schools.* The East London Research School. https://researchschool.org.uk/eastlondon/blogs/improving-social-and-emotional-learning-in-early-years-and-primary-if-not-now-when/.

Hammond, Z. (2015). *Culturally responsive teaching and the brain.* Corwin.

Head Start. (2020, April). Effective practice guides. Early Childhood Learning and Knowledge Center. https://eclkc.ohs.acf.hhs.gov/school-readiness/effective-practice-guides/social-emotional-development.

Horowitz, J. M. & Graf, N. (2019, February). Most US teens see anxiety and depression as a major problem among their peers. Pew Research Center. https://www.pewsocialtrends.org/2019/02/20/most-u-s-teens-see-anxiety-and-depression-as-a-major-problem-among-their-peers/.

Iaosanurak, C., Chanchalor, S., & Murphy, E. (2015, May). Social and emotional learning around technology in a cross-cultural, elementary classroom. *Education and Information Technology, 21*(6), 1639–62. file:///D:/Ed.%20Tech%20Book/SEL%20and%20Technology.pdf.

iGame Mom. (2020). 10 Apps helping kids develop social and emotional skills. https://ajph.aphapublications.org/doi/full/10.2105/AJPH.2015.302630.

Jager, R. J., Rivas-Drake, D., & Borowski, T. (2018, November). *Equity and social and emotional learning: A cultural analysis.* Establishing Practical Social-Emotional Competency Assessments Work Group. https://measuringsel.casel.org/wp-content/uploads/2018/11/Frameworks-Equity.pdf.

Jones, D. E., Greenberg, M., & Crowley, M. (2015, November). Early social-emotional functioning and public health: The relationship between kindergarten social competence and future wellness. *American Journal of Public Health.* https://ajph.aphapublications.org/doi/full/10.2105/AJPH.2015.302630.

Kemper, Ashley. (2019, June 23). *Common Sense Education.* https://www.commonsensemedia.org/app-reviews/social-quest.

Krach, S. K., McCreery, M. P., Doss, K. M, & Highsmith, D. M. (2020, January). Can computers teach social skills to children? Examining the efficacy of "the social express" in an African-American sample. *Contemporary School Psychology.* https://doi.org/10.1007/s40688-019-00270-z.

Krause, C. (2019, July 6). How tech is taking social-emotional learning out of its silo. EdSurge. https://www.edsurge.com/news/2019-07-06-how-tech-is-taking-social-emotional-learning-out-of-its-silo.

Kutnick, P. (1997). Computer-based problem-solving: The effects of group composition and social skills on a cognitive joint action task. *Educational Research, 39*(2), 135–47.

McGraw-Hill Education Applied Learning Sciences Team. (2017, November). Fostering social and emotional learning (SEL) through technology. McGraw Hill. https://medium.com/inspired-ideas-prek-12/fostering-social-and-emotional-learning-through-technology-8da6974e54bb.

Oberle, E., Domitrovich, C., Meyer, D., & Weissberg, R. P. (2016, February). Establishing systemic social and emotional learning approaches in schools: A framework for school wide implementation. *Cambridge Journal of Education, 46*(3), 1–21. https://www.researchgate.net/publication/292947112_Establishing_systemic_social_and_emotional_learning_approaches_in_schools_a_framework_for_schoolwide_implementation.

Rhodes, C. M. & Schmidt, S. W., (2018, November). Culturally responsive teaching in the online classroom. *eLearn Magazine, 11.* https://doi.org/10.1145/3295776.3274756.

Seider, S. & Graves, D. (2020, January). Making SEL culturally competent. *Edutopia.* https://www.edutopia.org/article/making-sel-culturally-competent.

Sesame Street. (2020). *Breathe, think, do with Sesame.* https://apps.apple.com/us/app/breathe-think-do-with-sesame/id721853597.

Sharma, S., Deller, J., Biswal, R., & Mandal, M. (2009). Emotional intelligence: Factorial structure and construct validity across cultures. *International Journal of Cross Cultural Management, 9*(2), 217–36. https://doi.org/10.1177/1470595809335725.

Shedd, M. (2019, September 29). Storyboard That: An exciting edtech tool that just got even better. *EmergingEdTech.* https://www.emergingedtech.com/2019/09/storyboard-that-exciting-edtech-tool-just-got-better/.

Social Quest. (n.d.). https://apps.apple.com/us/app/social-quest/id556089006.

Smiling Mind. (2020). https://www.smilingmind.com.au/education.

TeachThought Staff. (2020, July 26). 5 iPad apps for social and emotional learning. *Thought.* https://www.teachthought.com/technology/5-ipad-apps-for-social-and-emotional-learning/.

The Social Express. (2020). Social learning made easy. https://social express.com.

Torres, C. (2019, February 25). Social emotional learning won't happen without a culturally relevant start. *Education Week Teacher.*

Vygotsky, L. S. (1978). *Mind in society.* Harvard University Press.

W. N. (2019, July). Social emotional learning through classroom technology. *Go Guardian.* https://www.goguardian.com/blog/technology/social-emotional-learning-through-classroom-technology/.

Weird Enough Productions. (2020). *Get Media L.I.T.* https://getmedialit.com/.

Webber, S. G. & Wise, J. (2020, June). How would you feel it . . . Super Duper Publications. https://www.superduperinc.com/products/view.aspx?stid=630&s=how-would-you-feel-if—fun-deck-app#.XvUh1yhKg2x.

Zimmerman, E. (2018, December). Social-emotional learning competencies get a boost from classroom technology. Ed Tech Focus on K–12. https://edtechmagazine.com/k12/article/2018/12/social-emotional-learning-competencies-get-boost-classroom-technology-perfcon#:~:text=Social%2DEmotional%20Learning%20Competencies%20Get,engage%20learners'%20collaboration%20and%20communication.

Zins, J. E., Weissberg, R. P., Wang, M. C., & Walberg, H. J. (eds.). (2004). *Building academic success on social and emotional learning: What does the research say?* Teachers College Press.

Index

AAC. *See* augmentative and alternative communication
ABA Flash Card Emotions, 140
ABCYa! Word Clouds, 122, 123
Achieve 3000, 119
Acrobat Reader, 139
action research, 17, 19
adaptive switches, 111
adaptive technologies, 17
ADHD. *See* attention deficit
Adobe Connect, 139
Adobe Creative Cloud, 139
Adobe Creative Suite, 139
Adobe Flash, 139
Adobe Illustrator, 139
Anchor, 124
assistive keyboard, 95
assistive technology (AT), 95, 101–6, 108, 110–15
attention deficit (ADHD), 75
augmentative and alternative communication (AAC), 107, 108, 109, 110
autism, 46, 103

AutoRap, 125
Avokiddo Emotions, 140

Be Confident in Who You Are, 141
blogs, 30, 47, 55, 61, 83
Bloom's Revised Taxonomy, 90
Bloxels, 96
Bookshare.org, 105
Breathe, Think, Do with Sesame, 140

Canva, 121
CASEL. *See* Collaborative for Academic, Social, and Emotional Learning
Children's Online Privacy Protection Act (COPPA), 26, 27, 28, 29
child trafficking, 29, 31
classroom management, 39, 40
Code Academy, 92
Code.org, 91, 92, 94, 97
codeSpark Academy, 91
coding, 89, 90, 91, 92, 93, 94, 95, 96, 97, 98

cognitive disabilities, 110
collaborative community, 5, 21
Collaborative for Academic,
    Social, and Emotional Learning
    (CASEL), 134
collective efficacy, 41, 42
comic, 121, 127, 141, 142, 143
Comic Life, 122
computer science (CS), 90, 92, 93,
    95, 97
computer vision syndrome
    (CVS), 73
concept mapping, 58
conditional statements, 94
Connect, 144
COPPA. *See* Children's Online
    Privacy Protection Act
coronavirus, 30
correction log, 59
crowdsourcing, 54
CS. *See* computer science
Cubetto, 96
culturally responsive teaching,
    136, 137
culture of inquiry, 5, 16, 21
CVS. *See* computer vision
    syndrome
cyberbullying, 29, 30, 31, 74, 77,
    82, 83

data breaches, 28
data security checklist, 27
debugging, 93
digital citizenship, 31, 32, 79, 80,
    81, 83
Digital Citizenship Commitment,
    81
digital divide, 32
digital mapping, 58
digital natives, 54
digital portfolios, 61, 62
digital publishing, 61

digital safety, 61, 79, 82, 83
digital tattoo, 78, 79
digital writing, 54, 57
Draw and Tell by Duck, Duck,
    Moose, 121
dyslexia, 103

early adopters, 8
Edmodo, 127
EdPuzzle, 48
English language learners, 46, 60
equity, 32
Evernote, 127
Excel, 102

Family Educational Rights and
    Privacy Act (FERPA), 25, 27,
    29, 30, 32
FAPE. *See* Free and Appropriate
    Public Education
FERPA. *See* Family Educational
    Rights and Privacy Act
Flipgrid, 60, 123, 124, 144
Flocabulary, 124
4 Ts, 3, 21
Free and Appropriate Public
    Education (FAPE), 106
Free Online Wordcloud Generator,
    123

gaming, 69
gaming disorder (IGD), 75
Get Media L.I.T., 142, 143
Girls Who Code, 97
Google apps, 47
Google Digital Applied
    Skills, 92
Google Slides, 145
GSuite, 144

hashtags, 47, 54, 55
higher-order thinking, 58, 90, 143

Hour of Code, 97
How Would You Feel If, 144

IEP. *See* Individual Educational
    Plan
IGD. *See* gaming disorder
iLearn with Poko: Emotions, 140
implementation plan, 14, 15
Inclusive Technologies'
    HelpKidzLearn, 112
indexing, 54
Individual Educational Plan (IEP),
    101, 103, 104, 106, 113, 114
infographics, 120, 121, 127
inquiry process, 2, 9, 11, 16, 19, 21
Instagram, 54, 70, 77
International Society for
    Technology in Education
    (ISTE), 25, 26–27, 31, 81,
    93, 98
Internet use disorder (IUD), 76
iReady, 119
ISTE. *See* International
    Society for Technology in
    Education
IUD. *See* internet use disorder

Jiminy, 79

Kahoot, 117
Kind Foundation, 144

learning disabilities, 46
learning log, 60
LinkedIn, 46
Live Binders, 127
Lyric Lab, 125

Make Beliefs Comix, 122
mashup, 55
memes, 54, 77
metacognition strategies, 29

Microsoft Learning Tools, 102,
    103, 106
Middle School Confidential,
    133, 141
MindMUp, 58
Monarch Teaching Technologies'
    Vizzle, 111
motivation, 39, 40
multitasking, 67, 76, 77
Mursion, 45, 46, 48

net-etiquette, 31
nintendonitis, 74
nomophobia, 76

obesity, 73
occupational therapy/
    occupational therapist, 108,
    |110, 112
Office 365, 102, 106, 144
Osmo, 96, 97
Ozobot, 95, 96

personally identifiable information
    (PII), 27, 28, 29, 32
phantom vibration syndrome, 76
phone, 65, 66, 67, 68, 72
Photoshop, 139
physical therapy, 109, 110
PII. *See* personally identifiable
    information
Piktochart, 121
pineapple chart, 13
PIU. *See* problematic Internet use
Pixton, 122
PLC. *See* professional learning
    communities
podcasts, 47, 48, 58, 61, 128
Poll Everywhere, 125
pornography, 75, 76, 80
portfolios, 15, 61, 126, 127, 128
PowerPoint, 42, 102, 120, 145

Prezi, 58
problematic Internet use (PIU), 76, 78
professional community, 2
professional development, 4, 16, 18, 20, 21, 37, 43, 44, 45, 47, 48, 90, 105
professional learning communities (PLC), 4, 16, 17, 20, 21, 45

Quizizz, 125, 126

Real Friends *vs.* the Other Kind, 141
Roblox, 77

science, technology, engineering, and mathematics (STEM), 20, 89, 90, 112
Scratch, 91, 94
screen time, 68, 69
Seesaw, 126
SEL. *See* social and emotional learning
self-efficacy, 38, 39, 41, 42, 47, 134
sensory disorders, 103, 109
SETT Framework, 104
SEWB. *See* Social-Emotional Well-Being scale
sexting, 79, 80
SiLAS, 141
simulations, 45, 46, 48
Six Dimensions of Wellness Model, 71
SLP. *See* speech-language pathologist
Smiling Mind, 139, 140
Snapchat, 54, 70
social and emotional learning (SEL), 133–39, 140–46
social capital, 77, 79
Social-Emotional Well-Being (SEWB) scale, 72, 74
Social Express, 142

social expressions, 139
social media, 30, 31, 37, 44, 46, 54–55, 61, 66, 68–70, 74–77, 79, 83, 123, 127
social networking, 75, 76, 77, 81
Social Quest, 139, 143
Socrative, 125, 126
SpeakPipe, 124
speech-language pathologist (SLP), 107, 108
stalking, 75
STEM. *See* science, technology, engineering, and mathematics
Storyboard That, 145
students with disabilities, 32, 101, 102, 103, 105, 106, 111, 113, 114
Super Better, 139, 143
Superhero Comic Book Maker, 121, 122
Survey Monkey, 125, 126
switch, 107, 112

Tarheel Reader, 110
teacher burnout, 47
teacher inquiry, 10, 18
TEAMS, 144
technological pedagogical content knowledge (TPACK) model, 39, 40, 42
Tech Shoot-Outs, 18
texting, 76
TikTok, 77
TPACK. *See* technological pedagogical content knowledge model
trolled, 74
Twitter, 46, 55

UDL. *See* Universal Design for Learning
UGC. *See* user-generated content

Universal Design for Learning
(UDL), 101, 102, 104, 105, 106,
113, 114
user-generated content (UGC), 77

Venngage, 121
video coaching, 44
videoconferencing tools, 45
visual impairment, 109
Voice Spice, 124
VoiceThread, 60
Voki, 123

wellness, 67, 68, 70, 71, 72, 80, 81,
82, 83, 140
Word, 102
word clouds, 122, 123, 127
Wordle, 122, 123
word processing, 59
writing process, 52, 53, 56,
60, 62

YouTube, 65, 70

Zoom, 30

About the Contributors

Holly S. Atkins, PhD
Holly Atkins earned her BA, MEd, and PhD in curriculum and instruction from the University of South Florida. Prior to arriving at Saint Leo University, she worked as a middle grades English/language arts teacher. She is associate professor of education, chair of the Undergraduate Education Department, and director of the Teacher Technology Summer Institute at Saint Leo University. Dr. Atkins has engaged in more than fifty presentations and publications focusing on the meaningful use of technology in education.

Jessie Brown, MEd
Jessie Brown is a curriculum technology specialist at Nina Harris Exceptional Student Education Center School in Pinellas County, Florida, where she supports teachers and students in technology in all content areas. Prior to her role as a technology specialist, she was a self-contained special education teacher for thirteen years. She uses her experiences in the classroom to train teachers on classroom integration of educational and assistive technology.

Lin Carver, PhD
Lin Carver joined Saint Leo University with more than thirty years of experience as a teacher and administrator in K–12 schools (teacher, coach, and director), and as adjunct professor at various universities

prior to joining the Saint Leo University community in 2010. She currently serves as director of program approval in the College of Education and Social Services and program administrator for the Master's in Reading program. Her teaching responsibilities are in Graduate Studies in Education in the Reading, ESE, Instructional Leadership, and Education Doctorate programs. Her presentations, publications, and research focus on increasing student achievement through effective literacy instruction, engagement, technology, and educational interventions.

Elisabeth Denisar, MA
Elisabeth Denisar has been an English language arts teacher and instructional writing coach for almost twenty years. She is a National Board-certified teacher and was awarded "20 to Watch" by the National School Board Association. She has served as a fellow and technology liaison for the Tampa Bay Area Writing Project. She currently teaches English and AVID at Oak Ridge High School in Oak Ridge, Tennessee.

Nakita Gillespie, MA
Nakita Gillespie earned her BA and MA in elementary education from the University of South Florida. She is currently an adjunct instructor at Saint Leo University, helping to prepare the next generation of educators. Prior to joining the Saint Leo team as an instructor, she served as a codirector of the Teacher Technology Summer Institute while working in the role of learning design coach at Sand Pine Elementary School in Pasco County, Florida. Her career began as a K–5 teacher in Hillsborough County and Pasco County school districts. These combined experiences have allowed her to pursue her passion of supporting teachers in transforming their classrooms through the meaningful use of technology in education.

Lori Goehrig, MS CCC-SLP
Lori Goehrig is a speech-language pathologist with more than thirty years of experience in K–12 schools providing speech and language therapy to students with disabilities. She currently serves as assistive technology specialist for Pinellas County Schools, Florida, supporting teachers and service providers in determining an effective communication system for students. She also creates professional development focusing on the integration of augmentative and alternative communication within the classroom setting.

Rachel Hernandez, EdD
Rachel Hernandez began her calling as an educator, spending the last fifteen years of her public education career working with migrant students in low socioeconomic areas in Central Florida. She later went on to complete her master's degree, with the goal of becoming an administrator in Title 1 schools, working with economically disadvantaged students. In 2017, Rachel began working in higher education with a focus on educational technology and diversity. While completing her doctoral degree, Rachel continued conducting research on utilizing technology to bridge the achievement gap for minorities and students from low-income families, understanding the social and societal influences of middle school girls, the unique technological and educational needs of Generation Z, as well as addressing the digital divide in Title 1 schools.

Kimberly Higdon, PhD
Kim Higdon earned her undergraduate degree from the University of Texas, her MA in teaching from the University of Puget Sound, and her PhD in adult, professional and community development. Currently, she is a new teacher support specialist in Round Rock ISD and is an adjunct at Saint Leo University and Texas State University. Prior to that, Kim has served as director of reading intervention in the South Bronx and associate professor of education at Saint Leo University. In her thirty years as an educator, she has taught prekindergarten–eighth grade around the United States and overseas. Her passions are literacy, technology integration, and urban education.

Monice Iles, EdD
Monica Iles has more than twenty years of experience in public education as a counselor, school-based administrator, and an assistant superintendent in Pasco County, Florida. During her tenure she has focused on school turnaround and supervising high schools. She has experience supporting pre-K through FAPE 22. She received her bachelor's in psychology, a master's in guidance and counseling, and educational leadership, and a doctorate in educational leadership—all from the University of South Florida. She also serves as adjunct professor at St. Leo University in the Educational Leadership Department.

Maureen Kasa, MA
Maureen Kasa earned her MA in information and learning technologies with an emphasis in assistive technology from the University of Colorado. Her experience in special education and assistive technology spans more than thirty-five years and includes responsibilities as an educator, administrator, course designer, and presenter at the local, state, and national levels. Maureen is currently coordinator of assistive technology for the Pinellas County School Board located in Largo, Florida.

Madison McClung, MEd
Madison McClung is a Saint Leo alumna earning her undergrad degree in middle grades education with a focus in social studies. She went on to earn her master's degree from Webster University in education and innovation with a focus in mobile technologies. Madison has been working for the Diocese of St. Petersburg for three years as social studies teacher and instructional technologist helping students and teachers integrate technology into the curriculum.

Lauren Pantoja, MEd
Lauren Pantoja is a learning design coach at Paul R. Smith Middle School in Pasco County, Florida, where she supports teachers in technology and literacy in all contents. She earned a MAT from Webster University, which she has used during her more than thirty years as a K–12 educator and coach. She also designs and teaches courses for Pasco County School District to support teachers, and works as an adjunct instructor at Saint Leo University preparing future literacy teachers and coaches. These experiences provide the foundation, which has resulted in her recognition as Florida Literacy Coach of the Year.

Brandy Pollicita, MS
Brandy Pollicita received a BA from University of Nebraska–Lincoln and MS from Arizona State University in exercise science with a specialization in sport psychology. She pursued her passion for health and fitness as a corporate wellness manager for three Fortune 500 companies over a decade. She has been a certified group fitness instructor and personal trainer for more than twenty years with certifications from the American Council on Exercise, Silver Sneakers,

YogaFit, and the American Red Cross. She has taught courses in the exercise science department and the College of Public Health at the University of South Florida. She currently holds the position of instructor of health and wellness at Saint Leo University in the College of Education and oversees the introductory wellness course and various exercise leadership courses.

Made in the USA
Las Vegas, NV
17 January 2022

41644158R00105